The Provisioning of The Modern Army in The Field

Henry Granville Sharpe, Frank Atwood Cook

Copyright © BiblioLife, LLC

This book represents a historical reproduction of a work originally published before 1923 that is part of a unique project which provides opportunities for readers, educators and researchers by bringing hard-to-find original publications back into print at reasonable prices. Because this and other works are culturally important, we have made them available as part of our commitment to protecting, preserving and promoting the world's literature. These books are in the "public domain" and were digitized and made available in cooperation with libraries, archives, and open source initiatives around the world dedicated to this important mission.

We believe that when we undertake the difficult task of re-creating these works as attractive, readable and affordable books, we further the goal of sharing these works with a global audience, and preserving a vanishing wealth of human knowledge.

Many historical books were originally published in small fonts, which can make them very difficult to read. Accordingly, in order to improve the reading experience of these books, we have created "enlarged print" versions of our books. Because of font size variation in the original books, some of these may not technically qualify as "large print" books, as that term is generally defined; however, we believe these versions provide an overall improved reading experience for many.

THE PROVISIONING

OF THE

Modern Army in the Field.

BY
BRIGADIER-GENERAL HENRY G. SHARPE,
Commissary General, United States Army.

REVISED AND REARRANGED
BY
CAPTAIN FRANK A. COOK,
Commissary U. S. A.,
Assistant to the Commissary General.

1909
FRANKLIN HUDSON PUBLISHING CO.
Kansas City, Mo.

NOTE.

Upon my suggestion, Captain FRANK A. COOK, of the Subsistence Department, undertook a revision of "The Provisioning of the Modern Army in the Field."

It was his idea, in the revision, that by additions to the text and rearrangement of the subject-matter he could bring the volume up to date and make it adaptable for use as a book of reference, or a military text-book for schools, there being no American work which included a summarization of the varied and extensive literature on the subject. It is thought he has done the work well, and deserves full credit for the care, intelligence, and thoroughness which the revision indicates.

HENRY G. SHARPE,
Commissary General, U. S. Army.

INTRODUCTION.

In an age of such great activities as the present, and when so many books are being published, there should be some justification for adding to the number.

The fact that in this country practically no books have been published on this important subject would seem to indicate that the public and the service are both indifferent to the matter, except spasmodically when attention is drawn to it by reports of suffering. Periods of peace afford no opportunities for practical experience, and indifference to a subject indicates lack of familiarity, and this because the incentive to study and preparation has not been made imperative. This study, when pursued, must include all wars in all countries, and especially in our own.

The principal object of this small treatise is to give some idea of the difficulties of provisioning troops in the field, and also with the sincere hope that upon a fuller appreciation of these difficulties a greater number of thoughtful men may be induced to devise measures to overcome them, and at the same time ameliorate, if they cannot prevent, the suffering and horrors of war.

PREFACE TO SECOND EDITION.

The principles underlying the feeding of fighting armies have been absorbed by the writer during two years of duty in the Office of the Commissary General of the Army. During this period the facilities of a splendid library, presented to the Office by General Sharpe, and the privilege of free intercourse and discussion with him on the subject, have afforded the writer exceptional opportunity for acquiring some correct knowledge of the particular branch of the military service in which the Office is interested.

FRANK A. COOK,
Captain, Commissary, U. S. Army,
Assistant to the Commissary General.

WASHINGTON, D. C.,
    May 26, 1908.

CONTENTS.

	Page.
INTRODUCTION,	9
MOBILIZATION AND CONCENTRATION,	18
PLAN OF OPERATIONS,	19
BASE OF OPERATIONS AND OF SUPPLY,	20
PLANS FOR SUBSISTENCE,	20
CHARACTER OF SUBSISTENCE SUPPLIES,	21
INITIAL SUPPLY AT THE BASE,	23
EMERGENCY RATIONS,	24
RESERVES OF OVENS AND COOKING APPARATUS,	24
LINES OF COMMUNICATION,	25
RATIONS CARRIED BY AN ARMY,	27
RENEWAL OF SUPPLIES,	28
NUMBER OF WAGONS REQUIRED,	29
DEPOTS ON THE LINES OF COMMUNICATION,	29
RAILROADS AND AUTOMOBILES,	30
UTILIZING THE LOCAL RESOURCES,	31
STATISTICAL DATA,	32
METHODS OF OBTAINING SUPPLIES LOCALLY,	34
PURCHASES—CONTRIBUTIONS,	34
REQUISITIONS—BILLETING,	35
FORAGING,	38
DUTIES OF SUBSISTENCE OFFICERS,	39
THE MEAT SUPPLY,	41
FRESH BREAD,	42
ACCOUNTABILITY—PAPER WORK,	43

INTRODUCTION.

With the exception of Thiers, historians have devoted but little attention to the question of subsistence of armies in campaign, and it is difficult to find of record more than bare statements to the effect that an army has suffered from lack of food or that the special means for obtaining it had provided an ample supply. Explanation as to why the food supplies failed to reach the troops, or the details of the manner in which they were successfully collected, are lacking

Military writers on the continent of Europe, have, however, long recognized the importance of the subject. The work of BALLYET,[*] published in 1817, followed a few years later by the extensive treatises of Odier and Vauchelle, were practically the beginnings of what has become a vast literature on the subject of subsistence of armies in the field. The French have always been the leaders in this line of literature, yet, in spite of this interest in the subject and the attention they had devoted to it, their defeat in the Franco-Prussian War of 1870 and 1871 may be attributed in no small degree to the complete failure of their supply service.

This fact may be discouraging to the student of questions of supply; it did not discourage the French. Realizing their deficiencies, they made a determined effort to correct them, and, to aid them in the improvement of their system, they caused to be translated into French every military work of value published in foreign countries. From the best of their own and foreign writings on the subject of supply they have succeeded in evolving a system the equal, if not the superior, of any among the armies of Europe. So impressed by its per-

---
[*] "De la Constitution de l'Administration Militaire en France," Paris.

fection was Sir CHARLES DILKE, after witnessing the maneuvers of the French Army in 1891, that he wrote, in the *Fortnightly Review* for November of that year, an article on "The French Armies," in which he stated: "Germany has this year lost that uncontested supremacy in Europe which she enjoyed for twenty years."

The maneuvers of 1891 were held in a designated portion of the country, the arrangements being made in advance with great elaborateness. While the system of subsisting the troops in the field in those maneuvers was a great success, the officers of the French Intendance realized that in war they would not have the opportunity to make such elaborate preparations beforehand for the subsistence of troops in any particular region, and in the maneuvers of 1903 a new and greater problem was given the French supply officers to solve. The place of the maneuvers was not made known until just before the date set for the concentration of the troops, which consisted of two army corps, and then the Intendance was obliged to subsist those army corps from the resources of the country in which they operated. It was done in an entirely successful manner. With practice like this prior to the Franco-Prussian War, in connection with the theories of supply with which the French were already familiar, it is doubtful if they would have suffered the humiliating defeat which still rankles in the hearts of the French people.

The English have written comparatively little on the subject of subsistence of armies in the field, but that they are alive to the importance of it is clearly shown by the complete success of their supply system in the South African War. This success may be attributed largely to the organization in the British Army in 1888 of an Army Service Corps. "A Digest and Analysis of Evidence taken by the Royal Commission on the War in South Africa" states, page 110: "There are only two branches of the immense administration concerned in the work of taking the troops to the seat of war and of maintaining them there which came in for unqualified commendation, both as to the adequacy of their supplies and the capacity with which they were administered. One was the transport by sea, the other the supply of food on land." Page 249: "The transport by sea to South Africa from the United Kingdom and the Colonies of a force much larger than any which had ever crossed the seas before in the service of this or any other country affords a remarkable illustration not only of the greatness of British maritime resources, but also of what can be done when careful forethought and preparation is applied to the object of utilizing rapidly in war instruments which are in peace solely engaged in the purpose of civil life. If the same forethought had been applied throughout, there would have been little criticism to make with regard to the South African War." Page 228: "The evidence shows that both in method of distribution and in quality the supply of food was one of the most successful features in the South African War. Lord KITCHENER said (1901): 'I consider that the soldier was better fed than in any previous campaign. Complaints were few and far between, and the majority were of a trivial nature, which speaks well for the sufficiency of the ration and the general quality of the food supplied.' Lord METHUEN said (14,312): 'I never recollect the food supply and so on being better, or so good as it was in this campaign, from the beginning to the end. I have not one word to say against it.' Evidence to the same effect was given by numerous witnesses."

Nothing could better illustrate the importance or the result of careful study in time of peace of the art of subsisting armies in war than the contrast afforded by England's success in South Africa and her miserable failure in the Crimea half a century before.

Sir CHARLES DILKE, writing in the *United Service Magazine* (London) for April, 1890, said: "The last considerable war in which we were engaged was that fought out in the neighborhood of Sevastopol. It was a war which called less than usual for special cleverness on the part of those responsible for intelligence and for movements. There were no great marches, no skillful maneuvers in the open field at long distances from the base. Our most advanced posts in the Crimea were never a full day's march from the sea, and it would have seemed to be a simple task to provide for the army in the field. Yet the whole of our plan utterly broke down. The horses of the cavalry and artillery were destroyed by doing common transport work, for which they should never have been used; and the army of the richest nation in the world, commanding the seas, starved almost within sight of its own ships for want of proper arrangement as to food—rotted for lack of sanitary provision— and, from the absence of that care which is the business of a general staff, became a wreck of itself. Before and since, the character and endurance of officers and men kept the fragments together, and whatever pride we now take in remembering the struggles of the campaign is a pride in the endurance of the race when suffering the most unmerited and unnecessary hardships from want of brain direction. Carelessness at home in time of peace had to be atoned for by magnificent courage and dogged determination on the part of the soldier, at the cost of many lives. The miserable inquiry as to the conduct of the Crimean War brought into the national mind in a dim way the necessity for some sort of staff training, and caused the establishment of a Staff College, which has, on the whole, done much good."

The Civil War in the United States was fought from 1861 to 1865 with a larger number of troops engaged than had ever before been in the field. We find the following remarks made by Hon. E. M. STANTON, Secretary of War, in his annual report for 1865, in speaking of the Subsistence Department and of the manner in which the troops were subsisted in the field: "During the war this branch of the Service never failed. It answers to the demand and is ever ready to meet the national call."

President LINCOLN, during a visit to Richmond early in 1865, is reported to have said to an officer of the Subsistence Department: "Your Department we scarcely hear of. It is like a well-regulated stomach: works so smoothly that we are not conscious of having it."

General DE CHANAL, of the French Army, who visited the United States in 1864, being sent by the French Government to observe the operations in the Civil War, says, in his book entitled "The American Army in the War of Secession," page 200, in speaking of the Subsistence Department: "It would be difficult for a commissariat service to work more smoothly and certainly than does that of the American Army, especially as that army is unable to live upon the country and must carry all its supplies."

BARATIER, writing on the same subject, says: "If, from the military point of view, we cannot always admire the conduct of operations, we are nevertheless struck with the vigor and breadth of the views which directed the organization and maintenance of numerous armies, always supplied with immense means of action; we are likewise forced to praise the persistence displayed in the use of certain methods, especially pertaining to the matter of supplies."*

The voluminous reports published by the Government in what are known as the "Rebellion Records" contain nearly all the military correspondence on file in the War Department concerning the Civil War in the United States; and it is a significant fact that hardly any reference is made to the operations of the Subsistence Department.

The vast mass of literature that has been published relative to this war since its close has been concerned mostly with descriptions of battles, and, with the exception of General Sherman, no American military writers have made any extended reference to the workings of the Subsistence Department during that war; nor has any systematic treatise on the provisioning of armies in the field ever been published in the

---
*A. BARATIER, Sous-Intendant Militaire, "L'Art de Ravitailler les Grandes Armées," p 47. Cf "Puissance Militaire des Etats-Unis d' Amérique d'après la Guerre de la Sécession, 1861–1865," par F P. Vigo-Roussillon, Ancien Elève de l'Ecole Polytechnique, etc., Paris, J Dumaine, 1866, p. 65.

United States, except one elementary book on "The Art of Subsisting Armies in War," published in 1893, and the book of which this is a revision. The explanation of this would seem to be that the operations of the Subsistence Department during the Civil War were conducted so smoothly, as pointed out by President Lincoln and Secretary Stanton, that the importance of the matter has been entirely overlooked.

Following the Civil War frequent operations on the plains against hostile Indians led to erroneous notions as to the ease of subsisting armies. American officers in those operations obtained most excellent training in the duties of a cavalry screen of an advance guard of a modern army, but nothing more. Such officers, when drawing lessons from their personal experiences, may be disposed to think that all wars can be made somewhat after the fashion in which the operations were conducted against the Indians, when very small bodies of troops, rarely numbering over a few hundred, had to be supplied; and when of necessity, as the operations took place in a country devoid of provisions, all supplies had to be taken with the command. This fact must account for the impossible orders relating to transportation and rations published during the American War with Spain and their dissimilarity to those published at the close of the Civil War after the armies had been for four years in the field. The lack of Civil War literature, or other American literature relating to subsistence, and the erroneous lessons drawn from the personal experiences of officers on the plains, combined to produce practically a failure of the supply departments of the American Army in the War with Spain, which failure, had the war been of greater magnitude, might have resulted in a national disaster. After the formation of a General Staff and the establishment of a War College, the subject of supplies in war began to receive in the United States the consideration it demands.

Many of the famous captains of the past have recorded in their writings the great importance which they consider should be given to the subject of the subsistence of troops in the field.

Frederick the Great even made the assertion that the art of conquering is lost without the art of subsistence. In his "Memoirs and Instructions" he often goes into considerable detail, showing the care that should be exercised by a commander to insure the subsistence of his troops in the field. He has likewise incorporated this same subject in his poem on "The Art of War."

During the Peninsular War the Duke of Wellington was necessarily so much occupied with the question of food and supply that he humorously used to say that he did not know that he was much of a general, but that he prided himself upon being a first-class commissariat officer. (MAURICE, "War," p. 25.)

Military writers on the continent of Europe have pointed out that the failure of provisions is the greatest deprivation that can occur to an army; that it destroys discipline when it is most necessary, and that it can ruin the very best army in a short time. This is clearly shown in "Memoirs of Baron de Marbot," page 439. During the campaign in Portugal, a French sergeant, wearied of the misery in which the army was living through lack of provisions, persuaded about a hundred men to desert and become marauders. The sergeant gained the expressive, if contemptuous, name of "Marshal Stockpot," and his band became so bold and impudent that the French commanders were compelled to detach a force to storm their stronghold and exterminate them.

A few quotations from great commanders and famous military writers will serve to close this Introduction, which is written in an attempt to impress upon the reader the importance of the subject that is treated by this book:

"The art of conquering is lost without the art of subsistence."—*Frederick the Great.*

"The art of subsisting a body of men in the field is among the most difficult."—*Jomini. Quoted by Lewal in "Etudes de Guerre," p.* 4.

"It is frequently a more difficult task than to direct certain operations."—*General Foy, in "Etudes de Guerre," p.* 4.

"Famine is more cruel than steel, and starvation has ruined more armies than have battles."—*Montecuculi, in "Etudes de Guerre," p. 5.*

"The misfortune of lacking food and forage is the greatest that can befall an army, for it destroys discipline at a time when it is most necessary, and it may in a short time ruin an army."—*Guvion Saint-Cyr, in "Etudes de Guerre," p. 6.*

"A commander-in-chief expends, in our day, more thought in assuring subsistence to his troops than for any other purpose, and his best-laid plans are constantly being opposed and their effect lost through the lack of timely issues."—*Marmont, "Esprit des Institutions Militaires," Chapter V., p. 105.*

"Without regular issues of supplies nothing is possible. Their importance equals and even surpasses that of the plans of battle themselves. Before marching comes existence, and this requires food. Before fighting, supplies must be provided. After the battle the wounded require our care. The renewal of subsistence constitutes one of the gravest preoccupations of the military commander. It is a vital and decisive question, which he must not for a moment neglect, for success depends upon its observance."—*Lewal, "Etudes de Guerre," p. 5.*

"The difficulty of finding food for an army is one of the greatest difficulties of war. How is it that the most distinguished generals, who have seen their combinations fail in consequence of it, have not found its solution?"—*Marmont, "Esprit des Institutions Militaires."*

"In an army the commander is either all or nothing; unless he can control the auxiliary services, he will certainly be controlled by them. He must be either master or servant. There can be no other alternative." —*Lewal, "Etudes de Guerre," p. 18.*

"Nothing, in fact, that may contribute to the success of operations can be considered as beneath the rank or genius of the commanders."— *Thiers, "Consulat," liv. 4.*

"Mobility and power of action in an army depend upon a proper balance between its numerical strength and the available resources of the seat of war. Beyond a certain number, the strength of the army is but a load that crushes it. The want of food and forage strikes at discipline and hampers military operations. It must in a brief period weaken an army, particularly when it is engaged in making a long retreat."—*"Mémoires Militaires du Lieutenant-Général Comte Roguet," Tome IV., p. 641.*

"Men brought together in large numbers have wants; the talent to satisfy those with order, economy, and intelligence forms the *science* of administration."—*"Esprit des Institutions Militaires," by Maréchal Marmont, Chapter IV., p. 122.*

"Companion and sister of tactics, administration often anticipates

The Provisioning of the Modern Army.

and always aids, but never hinders it."—*Odier, "Cours d'Etudes sur l'Administration Militaire," Vol. IV., p. 298.*

"The great strategical movements of armies have depended always upon their means of obtaining food and warlike supplies."—*Colonel Maurice, "War," p. 13.*

"An army is a city flung down suddenly in the country, each day moving, each day requiring fresh alterations in the arrangement by which food is conveyed from the producer to the consumer. Yet this portion of the Art of War—one of the most important, *if not the most important*—receives but scant notice. 'War is the art of being the strongest at any given place,' and that portion of the Art of War that keeps the greatest number of bayonets in the ranks is surely not to be despised."—*Home, "Précis of Modern Tactics," p. 186.*

"An army must be fed, and many people rarely consider the magnitude of the operation. The action of an army in the field, its marches and its battles, the lists of killed and wounded, are what chiefly strike the eye of the looker-on; when a man is killed or wounded, or even when he is taken prisoner, his loss is chronicled; but the man is just as much lost if he dies or is invalided from want of food or medical aid. We read of so many guns and standards captured; but who notices the losses from privations and hardships? Yet the losses from the latter causes far outweigh those from the former."—*Home, "Précis of Modern Tactics," p. 186.*

"The feeding of an army is a matter of the most vital importance, and demands the earliest attention of the general entrusted with the campaign."—*General Sherman, "Memoirs," Vol. II., p. 389.*

THE SUBSISTENCE OF MODERN ARMIES IN WAR.

MOBILIZATION AND CONCENTRATION.

Before an army takes the field two distinct operations have to be effected—namely, the mobilization and the concentration. Mobilization is the act of putting troops in a state of readiness for active service in war. Concentration is the act of bringing together the mobilized troops at threatened points or at convenient points for taking the offensive.

The important advantages of assuming the initiative in a campaign have been so often illustrated in history that most of the great nations of the earth now have definite detailed plans for the mobilization of their armies.

"In 1859 it took thirty-seven days for France to collect on the River Po a force of 104,000 men, with 12,000 more in Italy. In 1866 the Prussian armies (220,000 in number) were placed on the frontiers of Saxony and Silesia in a fortnight; and in 1870 Germany was able to mobilize her forces in nine days, and to send in eight days more, to the French frontier, an army of 400,000 soldiers and 1,200 guns."*

"The system of mobilization of the German Army, the most complete there is, is no new operation; it dates from the 3d of April, 1809, and ever since then, when any change has been effected in the organization, a corresponding modification in the mobilization has been introduced. Notwithstanding that in 1870 some corps had completed their mobilization in seven days, and were able to commence moving toward the frontier on the eighth day, the German Staff is striving to re-

---
*VOYLE, "A Military Dictionary," third edition, p. 260.

The Provisioning of the Modern Army. 19

duce this interval of time, small indeed as it is, by one or two days."*

The construction of elevated roads in Berlin necessitated a complete change in the German plan of mobilization so as to gain a few hours in the execution of that operation.

Proper plans for mobilization include the storage at convenient points of a reserve of supplies and necessary arrangements for increasing the *personnel* of the supply departments, in order that the greater demands of the mobilized army may be promptly met. The methods of subsistence during the preparatory period of mobilization and concentration will not differ materially from those used in time of peace, but such changes as may be necessary in the application of those methods to meet the new conditions should be elaborately planned as a part of the scheme of mobilization. It is only when the period of active operations has been entered upon that the serious problems of subsistence begin.

PLAN OF OPERATIONS.

As stated by VON DER GOLTZ ("The Conduct of War," page 97), "A complete plan for enterprises in the field is impossible, because we have to reckon with the independent will of the opponent." It is, however, highly important that definite ideas be formed as to the object of a campaign, a fixed purpose, to the consummation of which the energies of the commander must be persistently directed. It is stated that Napoleon I. has made the assertion that he never had a plan, yet we see that all his undertakings were directed from the beginning at some large and definite object. A plan of operations can state what we desire to do and, with the means available, hope to accomplish, but the separate movements and enterprises to be undertaken to accomplish the object cannot be arranged in advance. The farthest range of a detailed plan can generally

---

*FURSE, "Mobilization and Embarkation of an Army Corps," p. 2. See also Bronsard von Schellendorf, "The Duties of the General Staff," Vol. II., p. 109.

not extend beyond the concentration. Thereafter much must depend upon the result of the first serious encounter with the enemy. But always the great general purpose must be kept in mind.

BASE OF OPERATIONS AND OF SUPPLY.

Consideration of a general plan of operations involves the selection of a base. Colonel MACDOUGAL, in his "Theory of War," explains that the base of operations is "the point, line, or district from which an army starts and from which all its reinforcements and supplies proceed when it is committed in a campaign. It may be a single town; it may be a frontier line of any length, or a line of sea-coast, if the army possesses the command of the sea; or it may be a district or a county, having breadth as well as length. Whatever be its nature, it must be such that the army retreating upon it, in case of disaster, shall, on reaching it, find succor and safety."

JOMINI, in his "Précis de l'Art de la Guerre," published in 1839, says: "The base of operations is most generally that of supply,—though not necessarily so, at least as far as food is concerned,—as, for instance, a French army upon the Elbe might be subsisted from Westphalia or Franconia, but its real base would certainly be upon the Rhine." However, at the beginning of a campaign it is difficult to conceive of conditions which would result in the establishment of one base from which the army is to proceed and another base from which supplies are to be forwarded to it.

Assuming, then, that the bases of operations and supply are coincident, it is evident that the base must be selected not only with reference to the military operations that are to proceed therefrom, but also so that it, as well as the army beyond it, can be sustained by all the resources of the country.

PLANS FOR SUBSISTENCE.

The general plan of operation and the base having been decided upon, it becomes the duty of the Subsistence Department to sketch out a plan of the measures which will have to be taken to insure the regular provisioning of the army. It must be shown how subsistence affairs are to be administered, the *personnel* required, the amount and character of the stores to be accumulated at the base, and the preparations that must be set going to furnish them and to renew the supply. Beyond the base, the plan of supply, like the plan of operations, cannot be arranged in detail. Much will depend upon the course of events and upon the resources of the theater of war. We should in peace tabulate and keep up to date the resources of all countries that are likely to become theaters of war, but it is wrong in principle to place any reliance, in the preliminary arrangements, upon our tabulated data. If, upon penetrating the enemy's country, it is found that its resources can be utilized, then the flow of supplies from the rear can be stopped; but the supplies must nevertheless be at the base, lest the resources upon which we have counted fail.

During the preparatory period, then, supplies must be accumulated and stored at various depots at the base, the amount to be stored depending upon the strength of the command and being independent of the probable resources in the theater of operations. This is practically all that can be done by the supply departments prior to the opening of a campaign, except that in time of peace, whether or not war is in sight, elaborate plans should be perfected for the organization of the service at the base and along the lines of communications, statistical data should be collected, and general regulations should be promulgated and mastered relative to the utilization of the local resources.

CHARACTER OF SUBSISTENCE SUPPLIES.

A ration is the daily allowance of food for one man. The subsistence supplies to be stored at the base will consist largely of the articles composing the national ration. The composition of the ration is governed by the national dietary, and varies in most countries according to the nature of the service to be performed. It is a principle of dietetics that the greater the amount of muscular exertion the more nutritive must be the food consumed. So that the soldier in war should, theoretically, have a better ration than when in garrison; but with large modern armies this principle has to be ignored, for the problem of the subsistence of such armies is practically a transportation problem only. The larger the ration the greater the amount of transportation required, and the greater the transportation the less the mobility and consequently the efficiency of the troops, for rapidity of movement is one of the essentials of success in war. Accordingly, we find that nations have adopted as the ration for campaigns one consisting of the most essential components of the peace ration, selected with reference to their portability, keeping qualities, and nutritive value. The less essential components are omitted entirely, and the quantities of the components used are reduced to the minimum consistent with affording a fair amount of nourishment. While the campaign ration is the one intended to be issued habitually in active service, it is recognized that opportunities will not be infrequent for increasing the issue to the full peace ration or even to a greater extent by means of supplies procured in the theater of operations or by shipments from the rear when the army is stationary.

There should, then, be stored at the base not only a liberal supply of campaign rations, but also an assortment of other stores ready for shipment forward to the fighting army whenever opportunity occurs, and for issue to the sick and at stations occupied by inactive forces. Upon the chief commissary at the base devolves the important duty of making a wise selection of these extra stores and an approximate estimate of the amounts required. Their issue to the fighting forces during any lull in the operations when transportation is available should be made with liberality, without strict adherence to the letter of the law. The commissary officer who hesitates to assume responsibility will surely be a failure.

Initial Supply at the Base.

The amount of supplies to be stored at the base will depend upon the number of troops and camp-followers to be supplied, but it would be an inexcusable lack of foresight to limit the amount by the actual requirements as computed. The complete uncertainty of war forbids it. The possible necessity for the prompt sending forward of heavy reinforcements before supplies can be collected for them, the loss of a supply train, the deterioration of stores, the capture, perhaps, of thousands of prisoners who must be fed, and other contingencies impossible to foresee, render it imperative that the depots at the base be stocked with a most liberal reserve of stores.

VON DER GOLTZ, in "The Nation in Arms," page 373, says:

"He who, according to directions, calculates the needs of an army in the field in pounds and provides for it according to the most careful dispositions, certainly will scarcely ever run the risk of a portion of the supplies he has furnished being spoiled. But the army will suffer by this arrangement. Two and three times as much as an army needs must be supplied, if it is to be kept from want; double and treble in respect to the good quality of the provisions, double and treble of the quantity."

And in the same book, page 374, CLAUSEWITZ is quoted as follows:

"The strength to endure privation is one of the noblest virtues in a soldier, * * * but this privation must be merely temporary, caused by the force of circumstances, and not the result of * * * a parsimonious abstract calculation of absolute necessity."

From May 1 until August 12, 1864, the daily average number of rations forwarded from Chattanooga to Sherman's Army, which numbered 105,000 effective men and 30,000 civil employees, was 412,000 rations—more than three rations for every man that left Chattanooga on that campaign. (SYMONDS, "The Report of a Commissary of Subsistence," pages 130 and 158.)

EMERGENCY RATIONS.

An emergency ration, as its name implies, is a ration intended to be used only on emergent occasions. It is a reserve ration, carried habitually by the soldier, who is not permitted to open it except by order of an officer or in extremity. The emergency ration has been referred to as "a substitute for nothing." Its greatest usefulness is on the firing-line, when, separated from their supplies, and with their regular rations consumed, the troops can, by using it, prolong the battle for twenty-four to thirty-six hours. The principal requirements of such a ration are that it be light in weight, of small volume, put up in a package of suitable shape for carrying in the haversack, capable of being eaten without any preparation requiring the use of fire, and readily procurable in large quantities in time of war; and it must provide sufficient nourishment to maintain the strength and vigor of a man for one day.

It is the duty of commanding officers to see that every man has an emergency ration when starting on a campaign. The Subsistence Department must store and maintain a reserve of these rations at the base and push forward a supply of them to depots within reach of the troops, with a view to the prompt issue of another ration when one has been consumed.

RESERVES OF OVENS AND COOKING APPARATUS.

Field bakeries are provided for in most of the large armies of the world, and for such armies it is important that a reserve supply of ovens and apparatus pertaining thereto be stored at the base, available for replacing those worn out or lost in the service.

Likewise a reserve of apparatus for cooking should be stored at the base, although individual cooking must generally be resorted to during the progress of a campaign. However, at the base, at depots along the line of communications, at hospitals, at permanent stations occupied by portions of the field army, and even at the front during inactive periods, such

The Provisioning of the Modern Army. 25

cooking apparatus comes in play. Cooking by organizations permits the employment of trained cooks and the preparation of more elaborate and palatable meals than is possible when each man cooks for himself. Moreover, it conduces to the contentment of the men and gives them more time for rest. Cooking by organizations rather than by individuals has always been the rule in the United States Army, but the reverse is true in most European armies. This probably accounts for the present enthusiasm of the German Army over their recently adopted rolling kitchen.

On account of the necessity of reducing the transportation of modern armies to the minimum, it will seldom be practicable or wise to carry cooking apparatus, even rolling kitchens, along with an army as a part of its authorized impedimenta. But a supply of cooking outfits should nevertheless be stored at the base, ready for shipment from there to such portions of the army as can use them.

LINES OF COMMUNICATION.

The supplies carried by armies are renewed either from the country invaded or by shipments from the base. The latter is the principal source of supply, and a commander is compelled, therefore, to maintain, at all periods of the operations, an uninterrupted connection with it. This connection is necessary, not only to enable him to draw his reinforcements and supplies therefrom, but also that he may return to it from the army everything which is likely to impair its mobility. The routes by which this connection is kept up, be they rail, water, or road, are termed the "lines of communications."*

---

*Cf. Clarke, "Lectures on Staff Duties." p. 52.
Wolseley, "The Soldier's Pocket-book for Field Service," fifth edition, p. 150.
Pierron, "Stratégie et Grande Tactique," Tome I., p. 323; also see "Ordinance of the King of Prussia," dated July 20, 1872, given in the same volume, p. 333.
Von Schellendorff, "The Duties of the General Staff," Vol. II., p. 237, et seq.
Von der Goltz, "The Nation in Arms," p. 377.

Along the lines of communication there will always be two streams flowing in opposite directions one of supplies and reinforcements from the base to the army; the other of the sick, the wounded, prisoners, captured arms, trophies, unserviceable supplies, etc., from the army to the rear. To feed and provide transport and accommodations for the detachments of men and animals passing along the line, without interfering with the transit of supplies to the army, is no easy matter.

The multifarious requirements cannot evidently be looked after by the commanding general of the troops in the field, but must be committed to the charge of an experienced officer, subordinate to the commanding general, with a sufficient staff of officers and clerks to assist him. This officer is usually designated as the "general of communications." His charge extends from the base of operations to the most advanced depot of supplies, inclusive.

The functions of the subsistence officer on his staff are to keep the base depots stocked with food, to furnish it to troops or others entitled to it moving or stationed along the line of communication, and to push it forward to within reach of the army in the field. His duties, it is seen, can be stated in a simple manner, but the performance of them requires administrative ability of a high order.

Baratier, "L'Art de Ravitailler les Grandes Armées," p. 156, et seq

Goodrich, "Report of the British Naval and Military Operations in Egypt in 1882," p. 208

Home, "Précis of Modern Tactics," pp. 193 and 194

Furse, "The Organization and Administration of the Lines of Communications in War,' the entire book.

"Etudes sur le Service des Etapes, d'après les Renseignments Personnels Recueillis pendant la Guerre de 1870-1871," par un officier de l'Inspection Générale Bavaroise des Etapes

NAPOLEON to his brother Joseph (Kaiserslautern, September 24, 1808): "According to the laws of war, every general who loses his line of communication deserves death By 'line of communication' I understand that line on which are the hospitals and hospital supplies, munitions of war, food supplies; where the army may be reorganized and regain, after two days' rest, its *morale*, which it may have lost through an unforeseen accident "—Pierron, "Stratégie et Grand Tactique," Vol I., p. 20.

The Provisioning of the Modern Army.

Rations Carried by an Army.

An army starting from the base takes along with it several days' supplies of rations, the number depending somewhat upon the nature of the service to be performed. Most nations fix the minimum number of rations to be carried by their armies, and allot to various units the necessary number of wagons or other transportation required to carry this minimum number, relying upon the theater of operations to furnish additional transportation if circumstances render it necessary to carry more rations.

The rations with which an army starts from its base are distributed:

1. On the man or horse;
2. In wagons or other transportation attached to small units;
3. In wagons following each division, far to the rear.

It is apparent that soldiers themselves should habitually carry at least the current day's rations; they should be to this extent independent of transportation, so that in the event of an unexpected encounter or a day's continuous march there need be no delay caused by the necessity of bringing up wagons and making issues. This principle is universally recognized, though the number of rations prescribed in various armies to be carried by the soldier varies. Another important consideration is the reduction of transportation effected by the soldiers carrying rations themselves. Consider two opposing armies of 1,000,000 men each, one of which requires the men to carry two days' rations, while the other seeks to relieve them of this burden and provides wagon transportation for all of its rations. The latter will require no less than 2,500 more wagons drawn by 10,000 mules. The problem of transportation for immense armies is a serious one, and nothing can be neglected that will reduce the amount required.

When combat is probable, the rations in the wagons attached to the units should be emptied into the men's haversacks and be refilled from the trains far in rear before the army proceeds to the encounter, for it is a serious thing to expose a supply train to capture by the enemy or to bring it up to the vicinity of troops in action. Their movements would be hampered, and great confusion would result in the event of a reverse and necessary retreat.

The wagons following in the immediate rear of different small units are variously designated and will here be referred to as "troop trains," suggesting their proximity to the troops. Those following far in rear of the divisions will be called the "supply columns."

RENEWAL OF SUPPLIES.

The continuity of the supply is habitually assured by the following method of procedure, which, of course, must be varied by circumstances: At the close of each day rations are issued from the troop trains to the men to replace those consumed during the day. The emptied wagons renew their supplies locally, or return half a day's march to the rear to meet a section of the supply train with rations, or await the arrival of the section, according to circumstances. If the rations are obtained from the section of the supply train, the emptied wagons of that section renew their supplies locally or return to the rear to refill. Because of the vast amount of transportation required for a modern army to carry even its minimum of supplies, it is now generally admitted by the best authorities that operations cannot, as a rule, be safely or successfully conducted at a greater distance than two days' march from the source of supply—that is, the supply trains should never be required to move more than a two-days' march away from the troops to renew their supplies. Also, since the wagons of the troop trains should be with their units, always available to participate in a movement, however unexpected, they should never be separated from the troops by more than half a day's march.

NUMBER OF WAGONS REQUIRED.

The number of wagons required to supply an army from the rear increases rapidly as the distance from the source of supply increases. The COMTE DE PARIS has furnished a remarkable calculation on this subject; he has shown that an army of 100,000 men with 16,000 animals, to move ten days' march from its base, would require 10,975 wagons of 2,000 pounds capacity each, drawn by 65,850 mules. He points out the impossibility of dealing with this number of wagons, and states that even if the distances be kept, the train would cover no less than 108 miles, which would be more than the whole length of the ten days' march.*

A calculation by a different method to show the number of wagons required by an infantry division consisting of 21,178 men and 7,785 animals, moving five days' march from its base and operating there, appears in the May-June (1909) number of the *Journal of the Military Service Institution*, in an article entitled, "Subsisting Our Field Army in Case of War with a First-Class Power." The conclusion reached is that the train must consist of 654 four-mule wagons, each of 2,500 pounds capacity.†

DEPOTS ON THE LINES OF COMMUNICATION.

If the army has advanced more than a two-days' march from the base, requisitioned wagons must be sent forward from there to within two days' march of the troops with a day's supply for the emptied section of the supply train. On account of the difficulty that will generally be experienced in supplementing the regular supply-wagons of an army by the necessary number of local wagons to carry forward each day a day's supply, it will ordinarily be found necessary to halt the army after it has proceeded two days' march from the base, or

---
*See Home's "Précis of Modern Tactics," pages 187 and 188.
†See Appendix.

at most three, until a depot of supplies can be established farther to the front.

Accordingly, we shall find, after an army has proceeded a distance from the base, a series of depots established along the lines of communications, about two days' march apart, the one farthest to the front being known as the "advance depot," and those between that and the base depots as "intermediate depots." The advance depot should be within two days' march of the army.

RAILROADS AND AUTOMOBILES.

Evidently the same difficulties of transportation will be experienced in moving supplies from the base to the advance depot, thence to the army, as in moving them directly from the base to within reach of the supply trains of the army; and the best authorities have therefore come to the conclusion that the lines of communication of large modern armies must be railroad lines, or occasionally navigable waterways, along which depots must be pushed as the army advances, and operations at any great distance from such lines of supplies will be impracticable on account of the difficulty of providing supplies by any other means.

The automobile may be developed into a most useful means of transportation for the supplies of an army, but automobiles can never replace railroads, and it seems probable that as the art of war and the art of subsisting armies continue to progress a corps of trained railroad constructors and operators must constitute an important part of the supply departments of modern armies.

"In a country with numerous lines of railway and vast quantities of rolling stock ready at hand there are immense possibilities of attack and defense, provided it possesses competent military force. Great bodies of men and material can be moved over extreme distances at very brief notice by a vigorous government, directed by the necessary skill and ability."
—*Holabird, "Transportation of Troops and Supplies."*

"It is thus evident that railways have become the true military roads of an army and that their location in the future will have a determining influence on the plans of campaign adopted."—*Michie, "American Military Roads and Bridges."*

"All countries have not adopted modern improvements, and in many railways either do not exist or are too few in number; but even in the most advantageous case, where these improved means of transportation are plentiful, an army requires also other means of transport on account of the constant shifting of direction of military operations, the destruction of railway lines by a retreating enemy, and the necessity to distribute the stores which the railways only carry in bulk."—*Furse, "Military Transport," p. 2.*

UTILIZING THE LOCAL RESOURCES.

In the petty wars of a great nation, occurring as they often may in a barbarous or barren country, dependence must be placed almost entirely upon supplies from the base; consequently such wars are often prolonged simply because the difficulties of supply render rapid movements impossible, but the modern wars of two great nations will seldom, if ever, take place in regions devoid of resources, and that army which, relying upon its base for supplies, fails to make use of those resources will infallibly be beaten by the one that uses them. On the other hand, to place exclusive reliance upon what can be obtained in the theater of operations would ordinarily be fatal, for the supplies of no country are limitless, and two of our immense modern armies operating in zones of limited area would soon exhaust the country round about and must then of necessity draw supplies from the rear. Armies continually on the move, tapping fresh supplies, might live on a productive country, but concentrate them for action and in a few days the available local supplies are exhausted.

It is therefore necessary at all times, even in rich countries, to continue to push the advance depot along, regardless of the amount of supplies that the army is obtaining from the inhabitants. The best plan of supply, then, is to live on the country if practicable, keeping, however, the advance depot stocked and conforming it to the movements of the army. French regulations, published in an order dated January 11, 1893, state the principle as follows:

"The country will be drawn upon as if nothing can be forwarded from the rear, but at the same time the trains and supplies will be organized at the rear as if nothing can be obtained from the country by the army."

In practice, the local resources will furnish most of the supplies when an army is spread out or moving; but when concentrated or stationary, the supplies must come from the rear.

STATISTICAL DATA.

In order to be able to take full advantage of the resources of a country, we should, in time of peace, make a careful study of the local wealth of such countries as may become theaters of war. Statistical tables should be prepared and kept up to date. As relating to subsistence, the data compiled should show the principal productions of the country, the distribution of the available resources, the importance of the last harvest, the kind and number of cattle and sheep in the country, the number, capacity, and location of flour-mills and bakeries, the means of transportation, railways, steamboats, and ordinary roads, the number of inhabitants, the character of the imports and exports. The necessity of considering the exports from a country in connection with the resources is well illustrated by the invasion of Lombardy in 1859 by the French Army. As large quantities of wheat were grown in that country, it was thought the local resources would largely suffice to provide subsistence for the troops; but it was found that the wheat had been almost entirely exported, wheat bread not entering into the ordinary diet of the people, and in consequence the French Army suffered greatly from lack of food. To supplement the statistical tables of a country we should note the most convenient foreign markets in the vicinity of each country from which we might make shipments to better advantage than from the home country. It must be remembered, however, that food supplies intended for the army are contraband of war.

The plan of campaign may often be influenced by considerations of the resources of the country, for the line of operations should, when practicable, lead through populous and fertile districts. The line of operations having been selected, supply officers moving along that line can often be materially assisted in making their requisitions, if supplied with detailed information regarding the resources. A knowledge of the resources will also effect shipments to the base. A hundred years ago NAPOLEON reprimanded his Chief of Staff, as follows:

"I think it ridiculous to send flour from Metz and Nancy to Donauwerth; by this means we shall end by getting nothing at all; the country will be overrun with transport, and enormous expense will be incurred. I will have none of these measures It would have been far simpler, in so rich a country as Germany, to get what was wanted by purchase. In twenty-four hours you might have collected as much flour and wheat as you could have wished I beg of you, Daru [the Commissary General], to make it clearly understood that it is my intention to bring nothing from France that can be procured in Germany."—"*The Line of Communications,*" Furse, *p.* 91.

Prior to the Franco-Prussian War of 1870–1871, Germany seems to have been the only nation to have devoted any considerable attention to the important subject of statistics, and it may be assumed that during that war that nation made full use of her knowledge of the resources of France, for it is stated that one-third of her supplies of food and forage were obtained in that country. While no attention had been paid to this subject in the United States until the present decade, SHERMAN states, in his "Memoirs," that he had in his possession, prior to his starting on the expedition that made him famous, detailed information as to the resources of the various counties of Georgia. It is well to reflect upon this bare statement of his. The French are now fully alive to the importance of this subject. Their statistical data relates to all matters affecting supplies and is systematically kept up to date and in great detail, and applied practically at her maneuvers.

METHODS OF OBTAINING SUPPLIES LOCALLY.

Supplies may be procured locally in three ways:
1. By purchase;
2. By requisitions;
3. By foraging.

PURCHASES—CONTRIBUTIONS.

The first is the preferable method, for the main thing is to obtain the supplies. By offering highly remunerative prices, the cupidity of producers and dealers will cause them to bring forward all their reserves Expense is of secondary consideration when the destiny of a nation is at stake. We can compel inhabitants to disgorge, but the proceeding is unpleasant; we incur the hostility of the people; delays will occur; and hidden stores may not be discovered. Moreover, if demands are made and the local authorities or the inhabitants refuse to comply with them, considerable embarrassment might result. We can, of course, arrest and punish the offenders; we can destroy public property, and seize what supplies we need if we can find them; but we can ordinarily get more supplies with less delay by the commercial transaction of peace-times—simple purchase. Cash payments facilitate the supply, and if available cash is not at hand, contributions of money with which to make purchases may be exacted from the local authorities. Demands for money will generally be found more satisfactory than requisitions for supplies in kind, for the collection is less difficult and the hostility of the inhabitants is not so apt to be incurred, also they bear upon the people in proportion to their financial means Contributions of money, moreover, are now recognized as one of the justifiable means of causing an enemy's country to feel more keenly the rigors of war, and may be levied on a town or community as a punishment. Contributions are not refunded.

The Provisioning of the Modern Army.

REQUISITIONS—BILLETING.

Requisitions are demands for necessary supplies or services made on the inhabitants, *through their civil authorities*. When money is demanded, requisitions are called "contributions." Requisitions differ from purchases in that the buyer fixes the price. They were first employed by Washington and so named by him in the War for Independence, and have since been universally recognized as a legitimate and useful method of obtaining supplies. Indeed, HOME, in his "Précis of Modern Tactics," page 182, says: "War cannot be maintained without requisitions on the people." And on the same page he quotes CLAUSEWITZ as saying: "Regular requisitions are undoubtedly the simplest and best method of feeding an army and are the only system that can serve as the basis of modern war." It is thought that Home and Clausewitz both intended to convey by these statements only the fact that subsistence from depots alone is impracticable in modern war; that supplies must be obtained also from the inhabitants. They appear to have used the word "requisitions" in a broad sense, overlooking the distinction that should be made between purchases, requisitions, and foraging.

Requisitions should be made on printed forms and, if practicable, in the language of the country; and if supplies are received on requisitions and not paid for upon delivery, a printed receipt should be given to the civil authority to whom the requisition is presented.

Requisitions may be made for cooked meals, in which case the civil authorities may assign soldiers to the various households in proportion to the numbers composing the families of the same. If the soldiers are also quartered in the same houses, they are then said to be "billeted" upon the inhabitants. In the enemy's country billeting upon the inhabitants may frequently be resorted to to advantage, especially by the independent cavalry, which, if dependent upon trains, would lose their mobility, and which must, to be efficient, live almost wholly upon the resources of the country. The advantages of billeting are that it gives the men a good opportunity to rest; they are provided with a varied meal; the food supplies of all kinds in the country are more completely utilized, and it is an economical method of supply. The disadvantages are that it causes great dispersion and separation of the different units composing the army, and, except in thickly settled countries, obliges a command to spread out over too large a portion of the country to obtain subsistence. The men, moreover, live in the kitchen, and are apt to demand, either by force or in other ways, more supplies than they are entitled to. Furthermore, many indignities are likely to be shown the female portion of the inhabitants of the country, as their natural protectors are, in many instances, enrolled in the ranks of the enemy's army. In addition, this method may lead to oppression on the part of the troops if they are not treated as liberally as they consider they should be, and it will provoke frequent disputes if more is demanded from the inhabitants than they should justly be expected to furnish. The dispersion of the troops prevents the officers enforcing strict compliance with orders, and is subversive of discipline.

Requisitions may often be necessary in the home country in a defensive war, though straight purchases can generally be made and are greatly to be preferred. The same holds true in the country of an ally. To enforce requisitions in such a country is a delicate operation, requiring the exercise of tact, judgment, and diplomacy. The whole subject should be a matter of mutual understanding between the two governments. Even in an enemy's country, requisitions should never be imposed in too arbitrary a manner. Before making any exactions, an estimate should be formed of all the resources which the inhabitants can be made to surrender without subjecting them to serious want.

"These demands should be imposed and apportioned with judgment and moderation, taking into consideration the population, the geographical situation, the nature of the products, the richness of the country, and also, when possible, proportioning the extent of the demands to the grievances of the conquerors. To ravage a country, you reduce the inhabitants to misery, to despair, flight, and then you not only deprive yourself of their favorable coöperation, but, on the day of reverse, you will find these same men implacable and cruel enemies."— *Vauchelle, "Cours d'Administration Militaire," Vol. III., p. 9.*

Private property and the person of the peaceable inhabitants who are citizens of the occupied territory should be respected, as war is waged against a state, and not against individuals.

The same rule applies to neutrals who reside in the country, but this does not exempt them from the burden of the requisitions or contributions. The occupying army can hardly be expected to stop to inquire whether certain stores are owned by a citizen of the enemy's country or by a foreigner, a neutral, resident there; such neutral by residing in the enemy's country has received a certain amount of security and protection from its government, and should therefore bear his full share of the burden imposed upon it by the war.

Some English subjects residing in France in 1870–1871 maintained that they were exempt from the requisitions imposed by the Germans. The English courts decided that they could not claim special protection for their property or exemption from the military requisitions and contributions to which they would be subject together with the inhabitants of the place where they resided or where their properties were located. (FERRAND, "Des Requisitions Militaires," p. 27.)

The method of subsistence at the front will always be determined by the commanding general, according to circumstances. If local resources are to be utilized, it will ordinarily be found best to conduct negotiations through the civil authorities if they can be found, regardless of whether purchases or requisitions are to be made, and the best plan is to tell those authorities what the army requires, requesting them to inform the merchants of the requirements, that liberal cash payments will be made, and that the supplies should be at some designated central place at a stated time, when the purchase will be consummated. In the event of a disposition on the part of the authorities not to coöperate with the army in the transaction, then the formal requisition should be served upon them, and such force as may be necessary should be used to compel compliance with the demand.

FORAGING.

Foraging is the collection of supplies from the inhabitants by impressment, *without the assistance of the local civil authorities*. Foraging is resorted to when there is not time or opportunity to address the civil authorities, or when they show a disposition not to assist in the procuring of supplies by requisition or purchase, or when the inhabitants are distinctly hostile or obstructive—in short, when, in the opinion of the commanding general, this arbitrary method would be productive of better results than any other. SHERMAN states, in his "Memoirs," Volume II., page 183, that his system of foraging was indispensable to his success in his march through Georgia; that the country was sparsely settled, with no magistrates or civil authorities who could respond to requisitions. And yet Sherman's method, successful though it was and in line with the methods of the Confederacy and with the practice of nations up to that time, could not be applied in its entirety in a future war. Under Article 52, Hague Convention, July 29, 1899, respecting laws and customs of war on land, supplies in kind procured from the inhabitants must be, as far as possible, paid for in ready money; if not, their receipt must be acknowledged. Sherman forbade the giving of receipts, although he authorized officers in charge of foraging expeditions, if they thought proper, to give written certificates of the facts. See Special Field Orders, No. 120, November 9, 1864, quoted in Sherman's "Memoirs," Volume II., page 176.

In his "Memoirs," Volume II., page 182, SHERMAN described his method of foraging as follows:

"Each brigade commander had authority to detail a company of foragers, usually about fifty men, with one or two commissioned officers, selected for their boldness and enterprise. This party would be dispatched before daylight with a full knowledge of the intended day's march and camp; would proceed on foot five or six miles from the route travelled by their brigade, and then visit every plantation and farm within range. They would easily procure a wagon or family carriage, load it with bacon, corn-meal, turkeys, chickens, ducks, and everything that could be used as food or forage, and then regain the main road, usually in advance of their train. When this came up, they would deliver to the brigade commissary the supplies thus gathered by the way."

The difference between requisitioning and foraging is clearly indicated in the following extract from General SHERMAN's letter of February 24, 1865, to General Wade Hampton:

"Of course, you cannot question my right to 'forage on the country.' It is a war right, as old as history. The manner of exercising it varies with circumstances, and if the civil authorities will supply my requisitions, I will forbid all foraging. But I find no civil authorities who can respond to calls for forage and provisions, therefore must collect directly of the people."—"*Supplemental Report of the Joint Committee in the Conduct of the War,*" 1866, Vol. I., pp. 331 and 332.

DUTIES OF SUBSISTENCE OFFICERS.

To properly supply subsistence for an army in the field requires a thorough knowledge of the different methods that can be used and an ability to select the best methods to meet the conditions prevailing. Upon the chief commissary of an army devolves the important duty of keeping his commander informed of the state of subsistence supplies, and making pertinent suggestions for the improvement of the service. His duties are wholly administrative. He should not be accountable for funds or stores, but should devote his whole time to the large questions of supply, leaving the details to his subordinates. Under instructions of the commanding general, he directs when, in what manner, and to what extent the country invaded shall be exploited to collect supplies, designating the zones of supply for each division. His duties keep him with his commander, but he must exercise, by means of reports from subordinate commissaries and such inspections as he can make, such supervision over subsistence affairs as may be necessary to secure efficiency.

The duties of the chief commissary of a division are likewise largely administrative. He should have money accountability and should be liberally supplied with cash, but should not be burdened with accountability for stores. He is responsible for the continued supply of the number of days' rations designated to be kept in trains and on the persons of the troops. He has immediate charge of the levying of subsistence supplies in the theater of operations, assigning to brigades their zones of supply, and transmitting to brigade commissaries the instructions of his commander concerning the collection of supplies and paying and accounting for them. He will ordinarily make payments himself for supplies purchased or requisitioned in the enemy's country, but may, if circumstances render it desirable, furnish necessary funds to brigade commissaries to enable them more readily, by payments of cash on delivery, to obtain needed supplies. In such case, if requisitions are to be made, he should generally furnish brigade commissaries with uniform schedules of prices.

Supply trains of divisions are, so far as subsistence supplies are concerned, under the supervision and control of division chief commissaries; but as these officers must of necessity be near their commanders in order to properly administer subsistence affairs, they should be allowed the necessary assistants for duty with the train.

Cavalry operating far in advance of the army or independently on the flanks will seldom be able to connect with the supply-trains of the army. Such supplies as they must take with them should be carried on pack-mules. A most active and intelligent commissary should be assigned to such cavalry with ample authority and cash to procure supplies. The commissary with the advance cavalry will often be able not only

The Provisioning of the Modern Army. 41

to procure supplies for immediate use of the cavalry, but also to make requisitions for or purchases of larger quantities to be ready for the army upon its arrival.

THE MEAT SUPPLY.

If beef cattle can be procured locally, full advantage should be taken of the opportunity; but to drive beef cattle on the hoof after an army, as the source of its meat supply, is an obsolete, objectionable, and now unnecessary expedient. The objections are many and are set forth in French, German, and Swiss official reports and by numerous celebrated military authorities in Europe. The "Dienstanweisung für den Schlachtereibetrieb und den Viehtransport" ("Regulations for the Slaughtering and Transport of Animals"), states that pigs, calves, and cattle, ready for killing, cannot undertake long marches, and that they can only be moved long distances overland by means of box-wagons. The "Regulations" lay down the distance that oxen can march in a day as 20 kilometers on the average, provided that there are two rest-days in each week and that the animals are well fed and looked after. Oxen and pigs will therefore have to be left behind when troops are continually advancing, and cannot, as a rule, be used in such circumstances for supply purposes. Any attempts to make the animals march farther might easily lead to the outbreak of all sorts of diseases. These animals have but little stamina; when they have to endure much physical exertion and are badly looked after and are insufficiently fed, they die and their carcasses poison the air. The conditions under which sheep can be forwarded are much more favorable. "The Regulations for the Slaughtering and Transport of Animals" gauge their average marching powers at 30 kilometers *per diem*. According to this, their rate of movement is approximately the same as that of the troops. Flocks of sheep could therefore be driven along and made use of for feeding purposes.

General SHERMAN states, as a result of his experiences in the Civil War in the United States: "In my opinion, there is no better food for man than beef cattle driven on the hoof, issued liberally, with salt, bacon, and bread." Military students cannot afford to ignore any conclusions of General Sherman's, but they must bear in mind that the Civil War was fought over forty years ago, during which period frozen meats and canned meats have made their appearance in the commercial world, and their preparation has been perfected to such an extent that in future wars they will surely be used to the exclusion of cattle on the hoof.

FRESH BREAD.

The supply of fresh bread to troops in the field is an important matter that has received full consideration by European armies, most of which have a field bakery column attached to their supply trains. The local resources will seldom be able to supply more than a limited quantity of bread to an occupying army, so that if soft bread is to be furnished, it must be obtained from large bakeries established at the base, or from bakeries accompanying the supply column. To ship bread from the base will soon become impracticable as the army advances, and the bakery column thus becomes a necessary adjunct of an army in campaign. Even with a bakery column, it will often be necessary to issue hard bread to the troops; but hard bread, on account of its indigestibility, will, if used as a steady diet, soon ruin the best of stomachs, so that advantage should be taken of every possible means of supplying fresh bread to troops in campaign.

The bakeries are usually established in rear of the supply train, near the advance depot. They should never be located nor the column moved so far to the front as to interfere with the mobility of the army; this is in accordance with the practice in European armies. Habitually, all the ovens of a fighting division work together, or if a division marches in several columns, the division bakery column should be similarly divided,

---

NOTE.—See Appendix for a discussion of the disadvantages in the use of cattle on the hoof.

and when organizations are detached for any purpose from their divisions, their share of bakery wagons should go with them.

If provision is made for a field bakery column, the details of its operation can, in practice, be worked out by the subsistence officers in charge. Detailed regulations should not be adopted, for the reason that the conditions of service will so vary—depending upon the local supply of bread, flour, or wheat, the length of the line of communications, the means of transportation available, the rapidity of the movements of the troops, the propinquity of the enemy, and other considerations—that much must always depend upon the judgment of the commanding generals and their subsistence officers.

ACCOUNTABILITY—PAPER WORK.

In time of peace a well-organized supply department has no occasion for rush, and the tendency of thoughtless officials is to prescribe a system of accounting so rigid and exacting as to impair the efficiency of the army if continued during war. To expect officers, when war comes, to burst suddenly all this red tape of accountability and assume the responsibility of prompt action, is not a logical sequence of such a system of training.

The aim should be, then, during peace to develop a simple plan of accounting susceptible during war of still greater simplification, and officers should be trained by theoretical and practical study in adapting the peace system to the conditions apt to obtain in war. Armies are maintained for the double purpose of discouraging war and undertaking it, and as the maintenance of large armies in peace, as well as in war, is an expensive proposition, it is undoubtedly justifiable and necessary to keep careful watch of public funds and property; but in war the red tape must be freely cut, else the supply officers must neglect their main duty, which is to feed the troops, in order to devote their time to the preparation of elaborate accounts

England's regulations contemplate that accountability shall cease at the advance depot, and the supply officers with the army are thus enabled to devote their time to their real business. Supplies proceeding from the advance depot are dropped as issued, and those collected locally and turned over to the troops or trains are reported to the advance depot for the necessary accounting.

APPENDIX.

1. Expeditions Beyond the Sea, ... 46
2. Embarkation and Disembarkation for War, . 52
3. The Number of Wagons Required in Front of Advance Depot, ... 59
4. Disadvantages in the Use of Cattle on the Hoof, 80
5. Bibliography, ... 93

EXPEDITIONS BEYOND THE SEA.

"Expeditions beyond the seas are all those enterprises in which large bodies of troops are conveyed in ships to a distant country, there to be landed to undertake military operations."—*Furse, "Military Expeditions Beyond the Seas," Vol. I., p. 2.*

"An expedition across the sea differs from other military operations, inasmuch as an army does not step over a frontier or advance from a selected base of operations, but is thrown into a hostile country, and all the combatants, materials, and stores have to be conveyed thereto from a distance in ships. Operations of this nature demand very thorough preparations, for, unless everything which relates to the number of troops, to the amount and assortment of war materials and stores, and to the quantity of provisions is carefully calculated, there is a risk of finding the means inadequate for the accomplishment of the object we have in view."
—*Idem, p. 84.*

In former times skill in handling and directing considerable bodies of men was thought to be possessed only by those who were connected with the profession of arms, and the French philosopher Helvetius was then probably justified in asserting that "Discipline is the art of inspiring soldiers with more fear for their own officers than they have for the enemy." In the commercial and manufacturing activities of modern times vast numbers of men are employed, and to direct them successfully a knowledge of how to handle, discipline, and control men is necessary. Modern business enterprises comprise every possible sphere of human activity, from the manufacture of the most delicate tissue for an infant's wear to the construction of the most stupendous works of engineering and the most formidable weapons of destruction.

War also is a business—that of fighting—and requires the application of business methods and principles, just as any other business does.

The supplies necessary for an expedition and the troops comprising the same may be represented by a large department store and its customers. A business man first constructs his store, next organizes his force of employees, procures and arranges his stock, and then announces his readiness to receive customers. The business of conducting a military expedition beyond the sea can and should be executed in like manner.

This discussion presumes that the command of the sea has been either temporarily or permanently gained by the Navy. It is not to be supposed that an expedition will be dispatched to make a landing at a place where the enemy has previously arranged defenses and concentrated a force to prevent the landing.

The command of the sea being assured, if a landing cannot be effected at one point, it can be at some other, and therefore business methods can be closely followed.

The preparation in peace for an expedition beyond the sea will include a profound study of the local resources of the country to be invaded, of the character of the harbors of same, the depth of water therein, whether adequate wharves are in existence or sufficient lighters are available, whether railroads run to the port, and the local means of transportation; and in particular this preparation should include compilation of full data of the size and number of vessels which can be utilized to transport the troops and stores, and the number of men, horses, wagons, guns, and stores that can be carried on each. The port of embarkation should be arranged beforehand, and an adequate depot with proper number of clerks and laborers established there.

The Japano-Russian War shows that the preparation for war should turn to advantage all the ordinary devices of modern social and commercial life.*

In all cases of expeditions beyond the sea there are four distinct phases—viz., $1°$, the embarkation; $2°$, the voyage; $3°$, the disembarkation; and $4°$, the subsequent operations.

---

*M. C. SULLIVAN, writing in *The Electrical Review* (New York, July 1, 1905), says:

"One of the most remarkable events that has occurred in the world's history is the battle of Mukden—remarkable because it was the mightiest land battle ever fought, and startling because no victory was ever won by such scientific methods. Feats were accomplished by the Japanese never before contemplated in war, and which had been previously declared by military experts to be impossible. The success of the victorious forces was almost entirely due to the skillful use of what is to-day considered to be one of the most ordinary and commonplace among electrical instruments—the telephone.

"From the sub-divisions of each portion of the army telephone lines were run to a portable switchboard, and from the various switchboards trunk-lines were run to headquarters several miles to the rear. Thus the parts of each portion of the army were made to correspond with the subscribers of a telephone sub-station in a large city, the headquarters being analogous to the central station, to which all of the subsidiary stations are connected by trunk-lines."

A transport, in a military sense, is a vessel capable of conveying a military unit fully equipped in all particulars and ready to take the field and engage in active campaign when disembarked.

To ship troops to invade a country in any other manner is as absurd as it would be to dispatch a naval fleet without guns or ammunition, with the expectation that these latter would be brought by other vessels and mounted on the war-ships when the enemy's fleet cleared for action.

In the British Army the amount of tonnage required to embark each unit of an army corps is carefully computed and published for the guidance of officers. The estimate is given in FURSE'S "Military Expeditions," Volume I., pages 210 to 215, inclusive. Such data should be computed and published for each of the military units of the country, the calculation being based upon the rule that each unit is to be embarked fully equipped with horses, wagons, etc., to take the field. Secrecy in such matters is only harmful and results in some officers not being informed fully of the duty required of them. On the other hand, it would be unwise to announce openly what vessels were available and the number of men, horses, wagons, and horse-boats each could carry.*

The vessels selected as transports are assembled at the port of embarkation and there equipped to receive the men, horses, and wagons. *Facilities for providing suitable hot meals for the men while on the voyage must be provided* An athletic trainer will not permit his squad to get out of condition when travelling to participate in a contest, and the condition of men who are to engage in a contest for the supremacy of their country should be as carefully guarded. Each vessel must be provided with supplies for the troops assigned thereon sufficient to last for at least ten days after landing, and with horse-boats and launches for landing the horses and stores.

---

*"In assigning the troops to the different transports, it is an admitted principle that, if possible, each transport should carry a complete unit with its regimental transport and baggage, or, if this cannot be done, that, at any rate, the portion of the unit carried should be complete with baggage, ammunition, equipment, stores, and regimental transport, so that it may be ready to land and act without reference to the remainder of the regiment or battery."—*Clarke, "Staff Duties," p 177; cf. Furse, "Military Expeditions," Vol I , p. 277; cf. Furse, "Mobilization and Embarkation," p. 195, and Furse, "Military Transport," p. 157*

"Testimony shows that the vessels were not loaded systematically. A battery with its guns and horses would be placed on one vessel and its

Materials, stores, and provisions, other than those embarked with the troops, must be shipped in the order in which they will be needed at the point of debarkation. It is a general principle that those things which are required first on landing should be loaded last.

The transports having been fitted and the stores shipped, the troops are brought to the port and each command placed aboard the transport *to which it has previously been assigned.*

The British Admiralty has ascertained that the maximum force which could be moved by sea at one time, without seriously interfering with trade or injuriously affecting the question of food-supply for England, is one army corps, a cavalry division, and the line of communication troops—in all 53,000 men, 20,000 horses, and 2,600 vehicles. (ROTHWELL, "Conveyance of Troops by Sea.")

"Taking the ships which happened to be available at a given date, and appropriating them by name to the troops of the 1st Army Corps, the cavalry division, and the line of communication troops, the transport authorities at the Admiralty obtained the following results: 134 ships, with a gross tonnage of 457,112 tons, would be required."—*Clarke, "Staff Duties," p.* 169.

This represents the maximum effort which the greatest maritime power in the world is capable of making. Considering the limited mercantile marine of other nations, the difficulties of transporting large armies across the sea will be apparent.

---

ammunition on another. The Second, Seventh, and Seventeenth Regular Infantry were each divided up and portions in each case sent on three different vessels."—*Report of the Commission to investigate the conduct of the War Department in the War of the United States with Spain, Vol. I., p.* 135.

"The First and Third Squadrons of the Sixth United States Cavalry were assembled at San Francisco the latter part of June, 1900, with orders to sail on the *Grant* July 1st to Nagasaki, there to receive orders for the Philippines or for China. About 250 horses had been sent to Vancouver to go on a horse-boat from there; the remaining horses left San Francisco July 1st on two horse-boats."

"* * * Twenty-five sets of the horse equipments of my troop had gone with that number of men to Vancouver with the horses of my troop and were to go on the horse-boat from there. When the order was received to place the remainder of my horse equipments on one of the horse-boats sailing from San Francisco with the horses of the other troops, I endeavored to get it changed. * * * For some reason this change was not allowed, and I sailed with my horses on one boat with part of the horse equipments, the rest of the equipments on another, and seventy-five of my men on a third."—"*Troop 'M,' Sixth Cavalry, in the Chinese Relief Expedition of 1900," Journal U. S. Cavalry Association, July,* 1904.

The Provisioning of the Modern Army.

Debarkations of a large force in a foreign country are of rare occurrence, and few officers study the complicated measures connected with the undertaking. Of recent years the British Government has endeavored to give officers and men some practical experience in this matter during peace In the British maneuvers of 1904, the fleet consisting of ten vessels, gross tonnage of about 71,000 tons, moved from Southampton and disembarked the troops at Clacton. Ten transports carried 559 officers, 11,139 men, 2,701 horses, 61 guns, 315 vehicles, 4 motors, 108 bicycles, and 54 horse-boats, and the maneuver demonstrated that this fighting force could, under favorable conditions, be disembarked in 10 hours, and in 24 hours sufficient transports could be landed to keep it in the field for about three days. In this movement the allowance was about 3 tons per man and a little over 11 tons per horse.*

As it will be necessary to establish a depot at the sea-base, it is advisable to assign one or more vessels for the purpose of transporting the stores. On this vessel should be sent the officers who are to be in charge of the depots, together with their clerks and laborers, and necessary mechanics and materials to construct landing-places and temporary depots. Agreements should be made with a competent railroad constructor to build a narrow-gauge railway at the base, and a vessel should be assigned to transport his men and material. A narrow-gauge railway known as the Decauville Patent Portable Railway is suitable for this purpose.†

The vessels having been loaded and the necessary horse-boats, lighters, and steam launches provided to accompany each, the convoy sails, escorted by the navy. Upon arrival at

---

*The following is now accepted as the allowance of tonnage, based on most recent experiences in war, of which any data is now available.

For voyages *over* seven days in duration and carrying three months' supplies for the command·
  Per man, 2¾ tons;
  Per horse, 8 tons
For voyages *not* over seven days and carrying one month's supplies:
  Per man, 2¼ tons;
  Per horse, 6¼ tons.

The above, of course, is based upon the infallible rule that units must be embarked complete in all particulars, including transport, horses, etc., and fully equipped for active service.

†The advantages obtained by the use of such a railway are well described by A. Perot, Sous-Intendant Militaire de 2e classe, in his work entitled "Emploi du Chemin de Fer à voie de Om. 60 pour le Ravitaillement des Troupes."

place of debarkation, the officer appointed to command the base should land first, together with his staff and the guard assigned to the base. Arrangements to provide suitable landing-places should be constructed, and when all is in readiness, the landing officer indicates what troops are to be landed, and as they reach the shore each unit is at once marched to the place assigned for its bivouac, which must be removed from the base. No troops are permitted to loiter at the base and none allowed to enter the limits of same without authority. Before disembarkation the troops are provided with field rations for several days and with one or more emergency rations. If several landing-places are available, the troops and stores can be discharged at the same time. Markers are established to indicate where each variety of stores is to be placed, and the stores are received and properly arranged by the clerks and laborers of each department. It is now known that practically the first articles unloaded by the Japanese at Chemulpo, in 1904, were small railway trucks, which were at once made use of in moving the stores from the landing-places. After the stores, troops, guns, horses, and wagons have been unloaded in this systematic manner, the command will be prepared to enter upon active campaign fully equipped with everything essential and with strong *morale*, induced by the knowledge that everything needed for their comfort and efficiency has been amply provided and systematically arranged at the base. That the foregoing is not an ideal, but a perfectly feasible, manner of effecting a debarkation is evidenced by the accomplishment of the Japanese at Chemulpo, in 1904, and represents an orderly, systematic, and business-like manner of conducting war, made possible by elaborate preparation of all the details in time of peace.

EMBARKATION AND DISEMBARKATION FOR WAR.*

"EXPEDITION OF UNITED STATES TROOPS FROM TAMPA TO DAIQUIRI, IN CUBA, JUNE, 1898.

"(Compiled from 'The War with Spain,' by H. C. LODGE, and 'Main Features of the Spanish-American War,' by Rear-Admiral PLUDDERMANN, Imperial German Navy.)

"In the spring of 1898 it was determined that a force of 15,000 should be despatched from Tampa, under General Shafter, to take part in the operations against Santiago. On the 7th of June orders were issued for an immediate embarkation, and, to use the words of an historian of the war, 'Then was displayed a scene of vast confusion. The railway tracks were blocked for miles with cars filled with supplies tightly shut up with red tape, at which men, unused to responsibility and to the need of quick action, gazed helplessly. The cars not only kept the supplies from the Army, but they stopped movement on the line, and hours were consumed where minutes should have sufficed in transporting troops from Tampa to the port. Once arrived, more confusion and widening of the area of chaos. No proper arrangement of transport—no allotment at all in some cases, and in others the same ship given to two or three regiments. Thereupon much scrambling, disorder, and complication, surmounted at last in some rough-and-ready fashion, and the troops were finally embarked.'—*H. C. Lodge, 'The War with Spain.'*

"On the 14th of June, after several false alarms of attack by Spanish torpedo-boats, the United States fleet got under way and crept towards its destination at about eight knots an hour—the limit of speed of many of the old steamers which had been chartered as transports. On arrival at Daiquiri, which

---
*From a gold medal prize essay by Lieutenant-Colonel C. E. D. TELFER-SMOLLETT, 3d Bn. South Staffordshire Regiment; published in the *Journal of the Royal United Service Institution* (London), April, 1905.

had been selected as a landing-place, it was discovered that the transports were provided with one lighter only for the disembarkation of horses and guns, and no launches. The one available landing-stage was but partially floored, and there were no materials or tools available for its repair or for the construction of other stages.

"Every boat and launch, even from the iron-clads blockading Santiago Harbor, was requisitioned for the service, and by the splendid efforts of the American blue-jackets, greatly aided by a spell of exceptionally fine weather, the infantry were got on shore during the first day of the disembarkation; two men, however, being drowned. In the absence of lighters or flats, horses and mules had to swim to shore, being simply hoisted out of the transports and lowered into the ocean; moreover, as there were no ordinary boats available to guide them to land, some fifty animals swam out to sea in the confusion and were drowned. Under the circumstances, it is not remarkable that the disembarkation of horses, guns, and stores was not completed for many days. The number of animals was very limited, as, owing to the omission to fit up a sufficient number of vessels for their transport, most of the cavalry horses had to be left behind at Tampa. The landing of provisions was effected with such slowness that the troops from the outset had to be placed on reduced rations; and throughout the disembarkation there was great confusion on the landing-place, which was congested with the men and stores, as no officer had been detailed to assume control there, or to act as base commandant.

"The disembarkation was practically unopposed, as the few Spaniards in the neighborhood of Daiquiri appear to have fled as soon as the American men-of-war opened fire. German authorities, however, are of the opinion that as the rocks reached close to the sea, and afforded many places screened from the fire of the war-ships, 300 determined men, although they might not have been able to frustrate the landing entirely, could certainly have inflicted very severe loss on the invaders. Great friction appears to have arisen between the military authorities and the officers of the transport steamers. 'The latter had only their own advantage and that of the ships' owners in view, and did not pay the least attention to the wishes and plans of the officers of the troops. The greater part of the time they kept at a distance of from three to twenty miles from the shore, * * * and if at times they did assist in unloading their cargoes, they would return to sea as fast as possible as soon as fire was opened ashore!' (Rear-Admiral PLUDDERMANN.) Even when the landing had at last been completed, the Army was wanting in mobility through the deficiency of land transport.

"Bearing in mind that the force engaged had been sent forth by one of the most powerful and most enlightened nations in the world, and that the descent took place at the close of the nineteenth century, it would certainly appear that the landing at Daiquiri is a unique illustration of the fact that even the most splendid resources cannot compensate for the absence of a well-established organization carefully prepared and tested in time of peace.

"The miscalculations and errors, which resulted not from individual incapacity — for all accounts bear testimony to the zeal and enthusiasm of American sailors and soldiers—but from an entire lack of pre-existing and established system, would have brought disaster to the very gates of the great Republic if its forces had been pitted against an enterprising foe. The forces of the United States have been without the schooling of war for thirty-four years; but it is not too much to say that the state of affairs depicted could not possibly have arisen if the theory and practice of the combined action of fleets and armies had been established before the encounter with Spain as a recognized branch of naval and military arts."

* * * * * * * *

"WAR BETWEEN JAPAN AND RUSSIA, 1904.

"(Compiled from the official dispatches and from the letters of the newspaper war correspondents.)

"One of the most detailed descriptions which has been published, on the authority of eye-witnesses of reliability, is that of the first disembarkation of the war, carried out at Chemulpo by a Japanese army consisting of 20,000 men, with 2,500 horses, several batteries of field-guns, together with an enormous mass of stores, estimated at 100,000 tons.

"On the night of the 8th February an advanced guard of 2,500 infantry was disembarked at a small existing jetty. On the 13th February, the Russian war-vessels *Variag* and *Korietz* having been destroyed at Chemulpo by Admiral Uriu's squadron in the intervening time, two Japanese transports arrived, carrying no troops, but filled with supplies and having Army

Medical Corps details and about 1,000 coolies for the land transport service. With the coolies came a carpenter corps of 100 men, each carrying his box of tools, and also an equal number of Army blacksmiths. These were detailed to put up a blacksmith shop close to the head of the landing jetty, and some of the carpenters proceeded to lay a cleated wooden roadway up the rough stone landing, to facilitate the disembarkation of horses and artillery.

"The Medical Corps of 300 hundred men came ashore in charge of the supplies for their own department: small trunks, weighing about 100 pounds each, containing necessaries for 'first aid' to the wounded, etc. The coolies were engaged in landing a vast bulk of military material, and nothing seems to have been forgotten. The Army authorities appear to have trusted in no way to local supplies. The advanced transports also brought 4 steam launches, 100 flat-bottomed boats, and 6 tank water-boats rigged with hand-pumps. During the next few days, under the direction of the Japanese military engineers, temporary landing-piers were erected, adjoining the permanent stone jetty.

"Wooden floats, which had arrived in sections in the transports, were put together, and cleated gangways were placed across and between them, forming a continuous floor with railings from the channel to land. Korean junks were also to some extent utilized in a similar manner. Whilst these stages were in progress supplies were coming ashore continuously. Some of the difficulties attending the landing at Chemulpo can be appreciated when it is understood that the mean rise and fall of the tide is thirty feet, and that for a considerable portion of each twenty-four hours mud flats, in many cases miles in extent, lie on either side of the narrow channel available for lighters and launches. The currents run like a mill-race. (All that can be said in favor of Chemulpo Harbor is, that it was better as a landing-place than the neighboring coasts.) On the 16th February seven transports anchored in the harbor and immediately proceeded to land men and horses. The flat-bottomed boats were taken alongside, the horses raised in slings, and lowered into them, each boat carrying five animals and bearing a transport departmental flag, giving its number and the number of the landing-float to which it was to go. On arrival at the float, each horse-boat was brought up broadside on; the troopers, holding the horses' heads, leaped up onto the floats, and the horses made the three-feet or four-feet jump from the bottom of the boat to the floor of the temporary landing-stage without hesitation or accident. A correspondent counted twenty animals landed in ten minutes, and one a minute would be a fair average, which was kept up for hours without cessation. Rice mats were thrown down to deaden the noise. At the same time two streams of men, fully accoutred, were pouring over two other temporary landing-piers, and the disembarkation of supplies was steadily maintained at the permanent stone jetty. Men and horses were rapidly marched to the adjacent railway station, where long lines of cars were in readiness to take them to Seoul. In spite of all difficulties, the whole force, together with an immense mass of stores, was thrown on shore in a space of barely a week without confusion or accident. At no time were the approaches to the landing-stages in the slightest degree congested, and all eye-witnesses affirm that men, horses, guns, and, above all, the immense bulk of 100,000 tons of baggage, were cleared away as if by magic.

"I have dwelt somewhat at length on the foregoing, because the details set forth give an almost ideal illustration of the perfection in the execution of naval-military operations which results on active service from methodical peace-training.

"The descent was completed within a few days of the outbreak of hostilities, and hence owed none of its success to the costly teaching of immediately preceding failures in the same campaign.

"In the years preceding the struggle the Japanese had, as a part of their unostentatious preparations, carefully organized and practiced a thoroughly efficient system of disembarkation, and when the day of trial at last arrived, this difficult and complicated operation was carried out with the absolute precision which is usually associated with the carefully rehearsed pageants of the Military Tournament at Islington.

"Everything was in its place, and every man knew what was required of him.

"Ample appliances and labor were at hand for the construction of new stages and the repair of those in existence, and it was thus possible to mitigate confusion by appropriating special and separate landing-places for the disembarkation of men, horses, and stores, respectively. A sufficient supply of boats was also available; and although the resources of even Japanese ingenuity have not as yet apparently been able to hit upon any more expeditious method of getting horses out of transports than by slinging them, yet the precision and method

which have prevailed have rendered it possible for this and the subsequent debarkations, which have been a feature of the war, to be effected with a speed and freedom from untoward events hitherto unsurpassed. * * *
* * * * * * * *

"It is possible that the prosperity which has attended the combined efforts of the fleets and armies of the Mikado may blind the general public in this country to the careful preparation and sustained effort to which the remarkable success achieved has been entirely due; and may lead to the impression that operations which have been carried through with such apparent ease cannot be difficult in themselves, that time and money need not, therefore, be devoted to the peace-rehearsal of such feats by our own forces, and that in the future, as in the past, we should fall back in such matters on the antiquated, dangerous, and costly policy of trusting to luck when an emergency arises. Now, there is no point which has made itself more clearly apparent than this: that up to the outbreak of hostilities the diplomacy of Russia had been very much in advance of her warlike preparations; whilst as regards Japan the state of affairs was exactly opposite, her rulers having been wise enough to let the work of preparation keep pace with the words of diplomacy. The whole campaign, therefore, has been a splendid example of the triumph in combined naval and military operations of method and peace organization over illimitable resources.

"But the lesson can be given in an even more concrete form than is afforded by the events of the present war standing by itself. If any man is inclined to doubt the correctness of the inferences drawn, let him carefully study the details of the Japanese disembarkation at Chemulpo, in February, 1904, and compare its features, one by one, with the similar operation which was carried through by the forces of the United States at Daiquiri, in June, 1898. The former episode was purposely selected for quotation in the first part of this essay, because it is an example of a descent executed with admirable precision, within a few days of the outbreak of hostilities, and consequently too soon for it to have been possible for any lessons learned during the existing war to have been applied. The disembarkation at Chemulpo, therefore, was a product of peace-preparation, and of peace-preparation alone.

"To fully realize the tremendous influence which national foresight may exercise as compared with numbers and wealth, it should be borne in mind that the forces employed at Daiquiri were engaged in executing the mandate of a great State, whose resources exceed those of Japan by many millions, alike in population and money. Yet, as we have seen, whilst the most essential appliances, such as horse-boats, were denied to the brave men of the United States forces at Daiquiri, at Chemulpo, in spite of the comparative slenderness of the national resources, every detail, down to signboards for the Japanese troop-boats and landing-stages, and rice mats for the horses' feet, were at hand and constantly available. The disposition of the British nation, like that of the Americans before 1898, and of the Russians up to 1904, has ever erred on the side of procrastination, where expenditure and preparation for national safety are concerned, and as a result, in almost every campaign, from the expedition to Carthagena in 1741 down to the present day, British sailors and soldiers, when called upon to uphold the national honor, have been placed more or less at a disadvantage, owing to the lack of previous peace-preparation Luck, sheer fighting power, the like unpreparedness of our opponents, have hitherto averted a catastrophe; but as years roll by the appliances for war become more complicated, and success is gradually tending to depend rather on scientific and systematic training than on personal courage. The immunity from disaster, therefore, which has hitherto attended our arms may, and probably will, fail us at a critical moment, if the object-lesson of Japanese foresight and Russian supineness be not taken to heart."

THE NUMBER OF WAGONS REQUIRED IN FRONT OF ADVANCE DEPOT.*

The present Field Service Regulations state that the number of rations carried by a command will vary greatly, but that the following may be assumed as the minimum:

1. On the man or horse, one emergency ration and one field ration;
2. In the regimental trains, two field rations;
3. In the supply columns, three field rations.

As to forage, each cavalry horse is required to carry a small reserve of oats—about six pounds. Forage for artillery horses, for quick supply, is apparently not provided for. The regimental trains carry two days' oats, twelve pounds per day for horses and nine pounds for mules; and the supply columns three days' supply of oats.

A proposed revision of the Field Service Regulations changes somewhat the above requirements and prescribes as the "normal" amounts to be carried:

1. By each man, one emergency ration, and in addition, when combat is probable or the troops are liable to be separated from their baggage trains, each man starts with two haversack rations;
2. In the baggage trains, at least two field rations;
3. In the supply train, three field rations.

On each cavalry horse, about six pounds of grain, and on each artillery carriage a small quantity. On the baggage trains, grain for two days; and on the supply train, grain for three days.

As a compromise, the following is proposed as the minimum to be carried in campaign by every division of the army:

RATIONS.—By each man, one emergency ration and one

---
*Extract from an article entitled "Subsisting Our Field Army in Case of War with a First-Class Power," published in *Journal of the Military Service Institution of the United States*, May-June, 1909.

haversack ration; in the troop trains, two haversack rations; in the supply train, three haversack rations. Total, six haversack rations and one emergency ration.

FORAGE.—By each animal or artillery carriage, one day's supply of oats (nine pounds per animal); in the troop trains, two days' supply; in the supply train, three days' supply. Total, six days' supply of oats.

It is assumed that when the command is forced to use the emergency ration, the animals must subsist that day by grazing. Thus an army supplied as above can subsist seven days on the supplies accompanying it.

It will be noted that it is proposed to substitute the new haversack ration for the field ration as the ration for campaigns. The desirability or necessity of the substitution will be demonstrated at the very outset of any campaign when one begins to figure on the amount of transportation required. The Field Service Regulations allot 81 wagons to the supply column of a division, prescribing that three days' field rations and three days' forage shall be carried therein. This number of wagons seems to have been adopted for no other reason than that the Germans have that number. It will be shown later that to carry even three haversack rations and three days' reduced supply of forage (nine pounds of oats per animal per day), more than twice that number of wagons will be necessary. As the field ration is half as heavy again as the haversack ration, it is estimated that 250 wagons instead of 81 would be required to a division if an attempt were made to carry along three days' field rations and three days' full allowance of grain. The number of wagons required at the advance depot and along the line of communication would be correspondingly great, and there is no doubt that any army commander would see at once the necessity of leaving behind such field luxuries as potatoes and onions, beans, jam, milk, etc., and settling down to the still difficult task of supplying even the practical haversack ration. It will be assumed, therefore, in the following discussion, that the haversack ration, and not the field, is to be carried by the men, by the troop trains, and by the supply train.

Of course, when an army becomes stationary, it will often be practicable to supply it with more than the bare necessities, but it is folly to attempt habitually to do so.

The proposed Field Service Regulations state that the men are required to carry rations (other than the emergency ration) only when necessary. As a matter of fact, it is always necessary for them to carry rations. Home, in his "Précis of Modern Tactics," page 178, in describing a movement of the Crown Prince's army during the Franco-German War, says:

"* * * When each column halted for the night at the places indicated in the orders, the head of the column did not halt there, with all the tail spread out along the road it had marched on, but each corps drew its tail up after it, and more or less formed a line of battle. Thus the roads were cleared, and it then became possible for the trains to advance with food. But it is manifest that if the soldier, having to march twelve to fifteen miles, and starting at 4 A. M., and probably not getting settled into his bivouac until 3 or 4 o'clock in the afternoon, had to wait for his food until the train arrived, he would be simply starved. Therefore, it follows that if troops are to be fed in the field, they must carry rations with them, and the rations consumed during the day must be replaced by the train during the night, so that the men shall move off the following day with the same number of rations as previously. *Soldiers, if they are not to starve, must carry rations.* No one who has considered this subject will question the truth of these words. * * *"

It will be assumed, therefore, that each soldier carries a minimum of one emergency ration and one haversack ration.

The trains accompanying the troops, following immediately after various units, are designated by various names in foreign countries, and have had numerous designations in our own, as, for instance, regimental trains, baggage trains, field trains. As being more descriptive than any of these, the designation "troop trains" is suggested and is used in this discussion.

We will now proceed to determine by a series of diagrams just what can be accomplished in the way of supplying a division at different distances in front of the advance depot with food and forage, assuming that each man carries an emergency ration and a haversack ration, each horse or artillery carriage a day's supply of oats, each troop train two days' supply of haversack rations and oats, and the supply train three days' supply.

We will assume first that a division is moved one day's march, say fifteen miles, from the advance depot, and that it is to operate there. Chart I. illustrates the method of its supply. The upper horizontal line represents the advance depot, the lower line is a day's march away. On the first of the month the army advances. During the first day's march, or after its completion, the men consume the one day's rations which they carried in their haversacks. The troop trains arrive later and issue a day's rations to the men for use the next day. Late at night one section of the supply column arrives and issues a day's rations to the troop trains. The other two sections of the supply column remain at the depot. On the second the empty section returns to the advance depot and the second section starts from there, arriving in the evening and issuing its rations to replace those consumed during the day. This movement is continued from day to day. The troops will therefore have three days' haversack rations with them at the beginning of each day, and the emergency ration. Two sections of the supply train pass each other every day, one going loaded, the

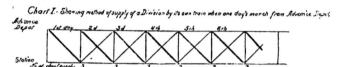

other returning empty. The remaining section with a day's rations is at the advance depot. Every returning section has a day's rest before starting again, transportation is ample, and there is no difficulty in supplying the army. But transportation should not be idle--that is, a day's work should be done every day. Forced marches are to be avoided, and continuous work without rest; but to rest thirty-six hours instead of twelve is inexcusable, unless it be to recuperate after a long spell of hard work. In the case under consideration, the three sections of the supply column should be made into two, and should carry full field rations to the troops, if practicable, instead of haversack rations, and should at least carry fresh bread and frozen beef if available. Advantage should be taken of the stationary position of the army to push forward supplies, including emergency rations, along the line of communications to the advance depot and to gather into that depot supplies procured from the country. The amount of supplies to be accumulated at the depot will depend entirely upon what are to be the future movements of the army. The field bakeries should be established near the advance depot, turning out a day's supply of fresh bread to be forwarded to the troops each day. The troop trains can be utilized, if necessary, to assist the supply train, moving out each day, meeting the supply train half-way and returning the same day; but the troop trains should never move more than half a day's march away, lest an unexpected move of the army become necessary during their absence.

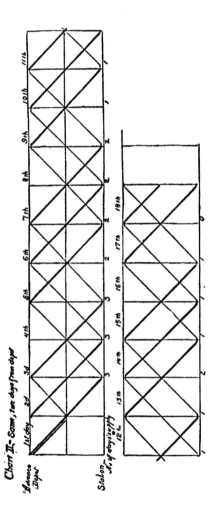
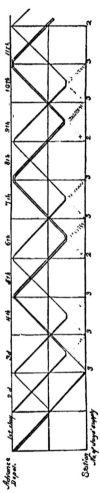

The Provisioning of the Modern Army. 65

It is evident that no trouble will be experienced in supplying with its own wagons an army operating one day's march from the advance depot, provided the depot itself is continuously supplied.

We will now consider a division operating two days' march from the advance depot. Plate II. illustrates the method of supply. Two days' rations are consumed during the march, therefore two sections of the supply column move out in rear of the army to re-supply the troop trains. The first section returns the second day and the second section the third day. At the beginning of the third day three days' rations are with the troops, and not counting the emergency ration. The supply is renewed the next two days by the arrival of the third section and the first section, the latter having returned to the depot and refilled, as shown on the chart. But on the fourth day no section is available to leave the depot, and consequently two days later no rations will arrive at the front and the supply is reduced to two days. Similarly, four days later (at the beginning of the tenth day) the number of rations is reduced to one, and on the fourteenth nothing but the emergency ration remains. Consuming that on the fourteenth, the situation is relieved by the arrival on each of the next three days of a section with a day's rations. But on the eighteenth no rations are forthcoming and the troops are without food. Similarly, every fourth day thereafter no rations are available. By living on three-fourths of a ration from the time of their arrival, the supply of three days' rations in the hands of the troops will not be reduced. It could be maintained also by requiring the supply sections to make forced marches, travelling twenty miles a day instead of fifteen, thus saving a day on the round trip.

The continuity of the supply when two days from the depot can, however, best be secured by utilizing the troop trains, as shown by Chart III. On the day of arrival at the station, one section of the supply column moves up to the troops and re-supplies the troop trains. On subsequent days the supply sections are met by the troop wagons half a day's march from the station, thus saving a full day's march for the supply sections, as clearly shown on the chart, and providing for a continuous supply of rations.

Thus at a distance of two days' march from the depot the question of supply with the prescribed number of wagons is comparatively simple.

Consider now a division moving three days from the depot

and operating there. Chart IV. shows the state of affairs. Supply sections arrive only on alternate days, and unless the troops are put on half rations, a continuous supply cannot be provided. It will be seen that on the ninth day the emergency ration must be used and on the eleventh day the troops will be without food.

If the troop wagons are used, rations can be obtained only for one day more, as shown by Chart V. If the trains make forced marches, rations will be forthcoming for a few days longer, but the transportation will soon wear out and the continuity of the supply cannot be assured.

It may therefore be concluded that more than the usual transportation will be required if troops are to operate three days from the advance depot. In the absence of additional transportation, arrangements should be perfected, before the departure of the army, for transferring the advance depot and the bakery column one day farther to the front; and the general principle may be stated that the advance depot should be within two days' march of the operating army, say within thirty miles.

As the distance of an army from the depot increases, so does the difficulty of its supply. It may often be impracticable to push the advance depot forward to within thirty miles of the active army, and in such case it becomes necessary to figure on the number of wagons required to supply it. This, in itself, is a complicated problem. Off-hand, one would say: Take the number of pounds of rations and forage required by an army each day, divide that by 2,500, the capacity of one wagon, and we have the number of wagons required to leave the advance depot each day. But, in order to carry forage for the mules that draw these supplies and rations for the drivers, more wagons would be required, and again more for the mules and drivers of these extra wagons; moreover, the returning mules and drivers must be provided for *en route*, and as the wagons return they again become available to send forward; so that we shall find great complications in the calculations and difficulty in arriving at just the number of wagons it is necessary to have at the depot in order to supply the army continuously.

The best way to solve all such problems is to begin at the end and work backwards. A complete solution of a transportation problem is illustrated by Chart VI., which will now be explained.

PROBLEM.—An infantry division is ordered to move seventy-five miles from the advance depot and to operate there.

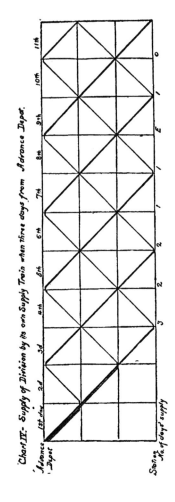
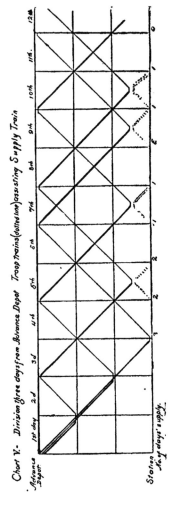

Chart VI. Illustrating method of supply of a Division moving and operating 5 days from Advance Depot.

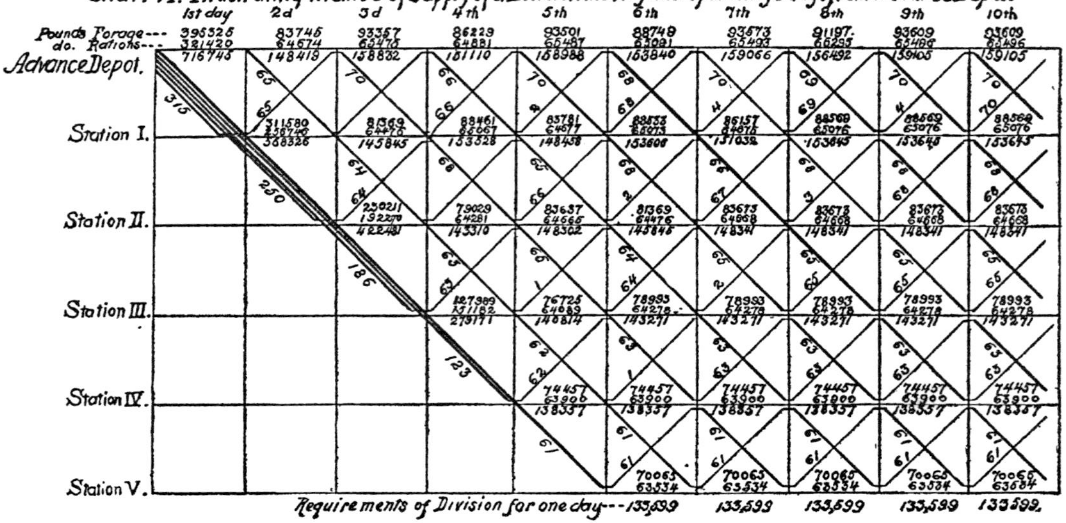

The Provisioning of the Modern Army. 71

How many four-mule wagons must be available at the advance depot to carry rations and forage for the division *en route* and to continue the supply after arrival? How many wagons must start each day, and how shall they be loaded?

Every night the supply train must issue a day's rations and forage to the troop trains to replace those issued by the latter earlier in the evening. Therefore, as the division is to march for five consecutive days, five days' rations and forage for the division must be carried by the supply train. Also forage and rations for the mules and drivers of the supply train. As each day's march is completed, the wagons that are emptied can return the next day toward the advance depot to bring up more supplies. Forage and rations for consumption during the first day of the return trip of these emptied wagons must also be carried along. To provide against accident, a percentage of spare wagons should be added. It will be assumed that 10 per cent spare wagons accompany the column. Some of these spare wagons can be utilized to carry extras, but all of them cannot be filled; otherwise when they were needed they would not be available. How best to utilize them, and what proportion of them should be loaded, will be explained later on.

To get at the total number of wagons required to accompany the division as a supply column, we will start with the last day of the march and work backward to the first. On the last day there must be wagons enough to carry one day's supply for the division and one day's supply for their own mules and drivers, also a second day's supply for these mules and drivers for consumption during the first day of their return.

The strength of an infantry division, exclusive of its supply column, as recently given by the General Staff, is 21,178 persons and 7,785 animals. A haversack ration weighs 3 pounds gross. Multiplying this by 21,178, we get 63,534 pounds as the weight of a day's rations for the division; and multiplying 7,785 by 9, we get 70,065 pounds as the weight of the forage; a total of 133,599 pounds required for use on the day of arrival, for which transport must be provided.

The capacity of a four-mule wagon is 2,500 pounds; but not all of this is available during this last day's march for carrying the supplies for the division. Each wagon must carry 72 pounds of oats and 6 pounds of rations, two days' supply for its own mules and drivers. We must add 10 per cent to this for the requirements of mules and drivers of spare wagons traveling unloaded, which gives 85.8 pounds. Deducting this from

2,500 pounds gives 2,414.2 pounds as the available carrying power of every wagon. Dividing one day's requirements of a division, 133,599 pounds, by 24,14.2 gives 55.34 wagons; add 10 per cent and we have 60.87 or 61 wagons as the number needed, plus 10 per cent, for the last day of the march, to carry rations and forage for the division for one day and rations and forage for two days for the drivers and mules.

We can verify this number of wagons before proceeding further.

Each wagon must carry 78 pounds for its driver and mules; multiply this by 61 gives 4,758 pounds, the requirements of the wagons; add this to 133,599 pounds, the requirements of the division, and we get 138,357 pounds, the total weight to be carried; divide this by 2,500, a wagon load, gives 55.34 wagons needed to carry these supplies. Adding 10 per cent space gives 60.87 or 61 wagons, as before.

For convenience of reference we will divide the total amount to be carried this last day into rations and forage, and similarly for other loads as they are determined, and record the results, so that by reference to the chart we can see at a glance just how many haversack rations and how much forage are with the supply trains at the various stations and as they start from the advance depot. The 138,357 pounds is found to consist of 21,300 haversack rations (63,900 pounds) and 74,457 pounds of forage. These numbers we record with the total, opposite Station IV. and under the proper date, and we also enter 61 on the diagonal lines as indicating the number of wagons carrying these supplies from Station IV. to V. and returning empty to Station IV.

We can now ascertain the number of supply wagons required to accompany the division from the third to the fourth station. Evidently we must add to the 138,357 pounds required for the last day three separate amounts, viz.: another day's supply for the division, a day's supply for the wagons travelling from the third to the fourth station, and another day's supply for those wagons which are to return empty the next day from Station IV. It will greatly facilitate the computation if from the 138,357 pounds we deduct the requirements of the 61 wagons for the last day of the march and include these requirements in the present calculation; for then we must provide exactly two days' supply for all the wagons moving from Station III. to IV., one day for the march from III. to IV., and a second day for those that proceed on as well as for those that

The Provisioning of the Modern Army. 73

return. The 61 wagons require for one day 61 × 39 pounds, equals 2,379 pounds, which, deducted from 138,357 pounds, leaves 135,978 pounds. We can now get at the requirements at Station III. by adding to 135,978 pounds a day's supply for the division and two days' supply for the wagons which are to leave Station III.

Add to 135,978 pounds 133,599 pounds, a day's supply for the division, and we have 269,577 pounds; divide this by 2,414.2, the available capacity of a wagon carrying two days' supply for its mules and drivers, and we get 111.66 wagons; adding 10 per cent gives 123 wagons required at Station III. Two days' supplies for these wagons amounts to 9,594 pounds, which, added to 269,577 pounds, gives 279,171 pounds to be carried by the 123 wagons. Of these wagons, 61 proceed and 62 return. The total weight is divisible into 151,182 pounds of oats and 127,989 pounds of rations. The results are recorded on the chart.

In making the above calculations it is desirable to keep the forage and rations separated, but the total amounts are referred to above in order not to complicate the explanation unnecessarily.

In the same way the weight to be carried forward from Station II. and the number of wagons required can be computed. Deducting from 279,171 pounds the requirements of 123 wagons for one day and adding a day's supply for the division, we get 407,973 pounds. Dividing by 2,414.2 and adding 10 per cent gives 186 wagons, the requirements at Station II. Multiply 186 by 72 to get the forage required by these wagons for two days, and by 6 to get the weight of the rations for the drivers, and add the sum of these to 407,973, and we have the total load at Station II., 422,481 pounds, of which 230,211 pounds are oats and 192,270 pounds are rations. Of the 186 wagons, 63 return toward the depot the next day and 123 go forward.

Similarly the requirements at Station I. and at the advance depot are computed. The results are shown on the chart. It will be seen that if it is intended to move a division five days' march from the advance depot and to continue its supply at that point from the depot, the division should be followed by a supply train of 315 wagons (10 per cent more than the actual number required), carrying 321,420 pounds of rations (107,140 haversack rations) and 395,325 pounds of oats. Moreover, at intervals of twenty-four hours, other trains carrying a day's supply for the division must start from the advance depot so that the amounts daily consumed by the division after their arrival shall be continually renewed. But before proceeding to find out the strength of these daily trains it will be well to verify the calculations up to the present time.

The requirements of the division during the five days' march amount to $5 \times 133{,}599$ pounds, equals 667,995 pounds. Reference to the chart shows that a day's supply must be carried along for the following number of wagons: $315 + 65 + 250 + 64 + 186 + 63 + 123 + 62 + 61 + 61 = 1{,}250$. Each wagon requires 39 pounds of forage and rations per day. Multiplying 1,250 by 39, we get 48,750 pounds, the requirements of the wagons; add this to 667,995 pounds, the requirements of the division during the march, and we get 716,745 pounds, as on the chart.

Again, the 315 wagons which leave the advance depot include 10 per cent spare. Therefore 315 is 110 per cent of the number of loaded wagons; hence 286 wagons are loaded. Dividing 716,745 by 2,500, a wagon load, we get 286 as the number of wagons required to carry this load. Q. E. D.

We are now ready to figure on the number of wagons and the load required to start from the advance depot on the second day in order to renew the supply at the front consumed by the division on the day following its arrival. As before, we begin at the end The number of wagons of this new column and the load required to go forward from Station IV. to V. are the same as before, 61 wagons carrying 138,357 pounds. The only additional wagons required from the third to the fourth station are those necessary to carry supplies for themselves during that stage and for such emptied wagons as must return the next day. Evidently the number of wagons that will be emptied will be small, and for the present we will ignore that number in order to discover better the available capacity of a wagon under the present conditions. From Station III. to IV. each wagon must carry supplies for itself for one day—that is, 39 pounds; plus 10 per cent, 42.9 pounds, which reduces the carrying capacity of a wagon to 2,500 minus 42.9, equals 2,457.1 pounds. Dividing the requirements of the last day, 138,357 pounds, by 2,457.1 and adding 10 per cent, we get 62 as the number of wagons required between the third and fourth stations. Of these, 61 go on and only 1 returns empty. This one returning empty must carry supplies for itself for one day, 39 pounds; but this small additional weight does not affect the number of wagons required, although the load of the 62 wagons must be increased by it. The 62 wagons consume 62 × 39 pounds of forage and rations, which, plus the 39 pounds for the returning wagon, equals 2,457 pounds; adding this to 138,357 gives 140,814 pounds as the weight of supplies to be carried forward from Station III.; dividing this into forage and rations, the results obtained and the number of wagons going and returning are recorded on the chart.

Starting now with 140,814 pounds as the initial weight to be carried forward from Station II., we can, by precisely the same method of calculation, arrive at the total load at Station II. and the number of wagons required. These are as recorded on the chart. Similarly, we work back to the advance depot, and find that 65 wagons must leave there on the second day, loaded as indicated.

The computations in the case of the wagons leaving the advance depot on the third day are somewhat complicated, due to the fact that returning wagons are met by this column, which must be supplied with one day's forage and rations for the next day of their return. But we shall find that approximately the same number of wagons arrive at and return from each of the stations, and by assuming that the numbers are exactly the same and making the necessary corrections afterwards, we shall have no difficulty.

The requirements at Station IV. are the same as before, and from this point on they are provided for by the wagons returning from the front the day before. That is, 61 wagons arrive at Station IV. from the front each day and the same number are required to carry supplies forward the next day. All of the wagons that leave Station III. on the third day may therefore return the next day toward the depot. The available capacity of a wagon is therefore reduced by its own requirements for two days, making it 2,414.2 pounds. Dividing the initial weight at Station III., 138,357 pounds, by 2,414.2, and adding 10 per cent, we get 64 wagons as the number required at Station III. All of these, after completing the day's march, return unloaded the next day. Two days' supplies for them amount to 378 pounds of rations and 4,536 pounds of forage, which, added to the initial weights, give 64,278 pounds of rations and 78,993 pounds of forage, a total of 143,271 pounds, to be carried forward from Station III. The same requirements for Station III. will be found to exist on succeeding days, and the chart for that day may therefore now be completed.

76   *The Provisioning of the Modern Army.*

Taking now 143,271 as the initial weight at Station II., dividing it by 2,414.2 and adding 10 per cent, we get 65 wagons required at that station. Of these, 63 go forward beyond Station III. the next day and 2 return; but 62 other returning wagons arrive at Station III. at the same time, so that the next day 64 wagons all together will return from Station III. and must be provided with a day's supplies. When we used 2,414.2 as a divisor above, we assumed that all the wagons to be used would require two days' supplies. It now develops that while 65 wagons go forward from Station II. only 64 return the next day—that is, in getting at the number of wagons we have overestimated the requirements by the weight of the supplies required by one wagon for one day; this is 39 pounds, which will not affect the number of wagons required. We must now add to the initial weight at Station II. the weight of the supplies required by 65 wagons for one day and 64 wagons for one day—that is, 129 × 39 pounds equals 5,031, which makes the total load at Station II. 148,302 pounds, of which 83,637 are forage and 64,665 are rations. Similarly, we work back to the advance depot and find that 70 wagons must leave there on the morning of the third day. As 65 wagons returned to the depot the evening before, only 5 additional wagons are required.

The columns of wagons which must leave the advance depot on the fourth and subsequent dates can be calculated in exactly the same manner. On the tenth we find 70 wagons leaving the advance depot and the same number returning in the evening; and we also find that between any other two stations on that day the number of returning wagons is the same as the number that leave. These numbers remain constant so long as conditions are the same We have then 70 + 68 + 65 + 63 + 61 = 327 wagons leaving the respective stations loaded each day; and the same number returning, or a total of 654 wagons required to supply continuously a division 75 miles away; this number is, of course, exactly the same as the number that have left the advance depot up to and including the tenth day, minus those that have returned to it; and, in general, on any day we can find the number of wagons working along the line by adding those that have left the advance depot and subtracting from the result those that have returned. Thus, during the fourth day 315 + 65 + 70 + 66 − 65 − 1 = 450 wagons are working along the line. On the tenth and afterwards the number is constant, amounting, as already shown, to 654 wagons. By means of the completed chart, the necessary orders for the movements of the various trains can be prepared in detail. The calculations have been explained at perhaps too great a length, but the importance of a correct understanding of the method used should be appreciated, for by this method alone can the amount of transportation required for a particular purpose be obtained with accuracy. The method is adaptable to all classes of transportation problems, and however many complications may arise in their solution, they can always be provided for if we bear in mind the point that we must always begin at the end and work backward. In the problem just solved it will be noted that no transport lies idle at any station, and none except the 10 per cent spare go forward empty.

It has been shown in the first part of this paper that a division cannot continuously supply itself from the advance depot with its own wagons if it is operating more than two days' march from that depot. In such case, the usual method is to send other wagons from the advance depot each day with a day's supply to within thirty miles of the troops, where they are met by sections of the regular supply train of the division. The same result may be accomplished as in the problem solved by increasing the supply train of the division by the necessary number of wagons. It can readily be seen that the number of wagons constituting the troop trains of a division may readily be fixed at such a definite number as may be necessary to carry two days' supply of oats and rations and such other impedimenta as may be authorized; but the number of wagons needed for the supply train cannot be fixed, for it must necessarily vary greatly, depending upon many conditions, as, for instance, the resources of the country, the nature and length of the communications, the distance of the enemy, and so forth. We can, however, readily determine the minimum number of wagons required to carry three days' supply of oats and rations for a division. The requirement of a division for three days amounts to $3 \times 133,599$ equals 400,797 pounds; and the requirements of each wagon carrying these supplies to 3×39 equals 117 pounds; the capacity of a wagon is 2,500 pounds, which, less 117 pounds, equals 2,383 pounds available for the division. Dividing 400,797 by 2,383 gives 168 wagons, to which 10 per cent should be added, making 184.8. As it is desirable to have the supply train divisible by 3, so that each section may carry a day's supply, it is submitted that 186 wagons should be the prescribed minimum allowance. Allowing 20 yards to a wagon, the supply train of a division, carrying only three days' rations and forage, will, if marching in a single column, extend over a distance of 2 miles and 200 yards. Of the 186 wagons, 96 are for forage and 90 for rations.

Referring again to Chart VI., it will be recalled that 654 wagons were required, which is 468 more than the number constituting the supply train proper of the division. In practice it is improbable that this number of extra standard four-mule wagons would be available—in fact, the transport of an army in excess of the prescribed allowance will ordinarily and of necessity consist largely of a heterogeneous lot of vehicles requisitioned from the country. In such case, the wagons should be divided into classes of approximately the same carrying power, and calculations as to the requirements should be made accordingly. By assigning the same class of wagons to the same stages of the journey, the calculations will not be unduly complicated. By beginning the computation with the last stage of the journey each day, when none but the four-mule wagons are used, we can readily work back to the advance depot. Eventually we will have 122 of the 186 wagons constituting the division supply train proper working back and forth over the last stage of the route and the rest between Stations IV. and V.—in other words, none of the regular wagons will be required to move more than two stations away from the troops.

Let us consider now what use should be made of the 10 per cent spare wagons provided. If a wagon breaks down we must have a spare one in which to load its supplies; so that, although it is desirable to carry extra supplies, all the wagons must not be loaded. By placing the computed loads at the advance depot on the wagons provided and then loading half the remaining wagons we can carry forward 5 per cent additional supplies. Of what they should consist will depend entirely upon the conditions. The most important extras to furnish troops are fresh beef or canned meats, fresh bread, some form of anti-scorbutics, preferably fresh vegetables, and tobacco. It may, however, be considered necessary to load the spare wagons with extra haversack rations and oats only. Unless the weather is suitable, it will be difficult to supply fresh beef or fresh vegetables from the advance depot, even if they can be gotten that far to the front; and to attempt to supply fresh bread by wagons to troops seventy-five miles away is, of course, out of the question. To the American soldier tobacco is more of a necessity thàn a luxury, and every effort should be made to provide it for sale or as an extra issue. It would be well, then,

The Provisioning of the Modern Army.

if practicable, to send forward a supply of tobacco at intervals. But as to other extras, everything will depend upon conditions, principally upon the resources of the country, the ease of supply of the advance depot, and the climate.

So far we have considered only the question of supply of an army from the advance depot when the army has moved a given distance from there and halted, and we have demonstrated a method by which the number of wagons needed to supply such an army can be calculated. Suppose now it is attempted to supply wholly from the rear an army that starts out with no intention of halting. Evidently it can subsist only for the number of days that the supplies carried with it will last, for there are no means of renewal. Starting out with say ten days' supplies, at the end of that time the army will be without food, ten days away from its point of supply. Then, if provision has not been made to supply it at that distance from the depot, the army can remain halted, or march on, or struggle back, but, whatever else happens, it will most likely starve, and it will certainly not be in condition to win any battle. The conclusion, then, is obvious, that an army dependent upon its base for supplies cannot start out on any expedition of indefinite length. Provision must be made in advance for keeping it supplied, and in order to make such provision the maximum distance it can go with the transportation available must be determined, and the whole transportation problem solved by the method that has been explained. Then if the army must proceed still further forward, the advance depot must first be pushed along to its vicinity, when it will be able to make another advance movement of fixed duration Thus, slowly, the enemy's country can be penetrated and contact with him be eventually secured.

DISADVANTAGES IN THE USE OF CATTLE ON THE HOOF AS BEEF SUPPLY OF AN ARMY IN THE FIELD.

As Shown by French, German, and Swiss Official Reports, and by Celebrated Military Writers in Europe.

Colonel FEISS and Lieutenant-Colonel GOOD, of the Swiss Army, were attached to the German Army of occupation in France in 1871, and submitted a report to their Government on "The Organization and Operation of the Subsistence Service in the German Army during the War of 1870–1871," in which report it is stated:

"In France, the German armies, during their forward movements, always found fresh meat sufficient for several days. This fact and that of the cattle plague, which had broken out in the herds brought from Russia, have impressed the most capable German intendants with the conviction that to drive cattle with the army is a great mistake. The cattle soon become mere skeletons; they catch and spread all contagious diseases; and finally it becomes necessary to kill them without their being available for the alimentation of the troops. It is for these reasons, gained from experience, that the German Intendence has, in the War of 1870–1871, founded establishments to make meat preserves by different processes."—*Pierron, "Stratégie et Grande Tactique," Vol. III., p. 15.*

Captain SCHAEFFER, in his "History of the Franco-German War of 1870–1871," edited by the historical section of the Prussian Great General Staff, says:

"But, at that time, the cattle plague broke out, which occasioned great difficulties for the subsistence service. The Chief Intendant of the Army was forced to adopt stringent methods in order to prevent this plague from spreading in the herds on the march. Orders were issued to slaughter all the cattle engaged in the direction of Landau–Nancy, to salt the meat known to be healthy, and to bury that which was contaminated. The introduction of cattle from Russia and from Austria-Hungary was prohibited; only the cattle from France, Belgium, and Holland could be drawn upon. Later, it was necessary to prohibit all importation.

"Notwithstanding all these precautions, cases of the cattle plague occurred constantly, which rendered the supply of meat and the variety in the food-supply extremely difficult. Recourse was then made to salt meat and to canned meats, for which they had had the forethought to establish a factory at Mayence, as well as to mutton; and it was possible to partly remedy the difficulties."—*Pierron, "Stratégie et Grande Tactique," Vol. III., p.* 40.

L'Intendant-Général FRIANT, 1874:

"The Prussians are now providing supplies of canned meats, having recognized from experience in the War of 1870-1871 the inconveniences occasioned by the herds of cattle, which are soon decimated by the cattle plague. There was presented to the Superior Commission of Subsistence, at Paris, of which I am the President, some canned beef, of excellent quality, good keeping properties, and very reasonable price. It can be eaten cold or made into soup. What economy would be effected if finally it was decided to adopt it and to comply with the general desire for a war food! A steer of 600 kilograms gross weight yields 300 kilograms of uncooked meat, and 300 kilograms of uncooked meat produce only 150 kilograms of edible meat. There would be no more loss from the frightful mortality among the herds of animals, and tainted meat would no longer be issued, which caused, in my opinion, sickness among the men. What kind of food can be obtained from cattle constantly on the move and which are not sufficiently nourished and soon become mere skin and bones, as in the Crimea in 1854-55? At Besançon, when Bourbaki's army retreated, in 1871, we lost 1,200 head of cattle from the cattle plague. In the Crimea, how many did we lose? A kilogram of meat supplied from cattle on the hoof becomes very expensive. It cost, on account of the losses, more than 15 francs in the Crimea. Forage, a valuable article in an army, and still more so in fortified places, is necessary for cattle on the hoof, and frequently there is not enough for such purpose."—*Pierron, "Stratégie et Grande Tactique," Vol. III., p.* 62.

A Prussian officer:

"Assigned to the command of the fortress artillery of Sedan after the capitulation of that fortress (September, 1870), and returning from Coblentz to my station, I met on the road large convoys of cattle destined for our army and on the way to Metz. They had only a single ration of forage, and moreover they were on the road for four or five days because of the obstruction of the railways.

"Arriving at Sedan, I ascertained from the commandant of the fortress that five thousand head of cattle, being forwarded from Belgium to the German Army around Paris, were to remain for some time in my care. In addition to the difficulty of corralling them, the difficulty of feeding them seemed insurmountable; this herd would have consumed in three days all the forage for the horses of the fortress. On my advice, they were placed on an island in the Meuse, which the animals could scarcely reach by means of a ford. In three days they had exhausted all the grass in the country, which became a slough. The water, because of a freshet in the river, threatened to submerge the island, and the situation seemed inextricable, when fortunately an order was received to slaughter the cattle, because of the cattle plague which had broken out in the herds of cattle of the army around Paris, and to forward to that army such of the dressed meat as was known to be healthy.

"These instances show what insurmountable difficulties are occasioned by the transport of such a large number of cattle on the hoof, difficulties which will only augment as the effective strength of modern armies is increased.

"To provide for the subsistence of armies in the field there is no longer any other practical method than the following: To have only such cattle on the hoof as can be provided from the local resources, and to exclude from the roads the live cattle.

"This method of transporting cattle on the hoof is an evident anachronism. It dates from the time when, lacking means for keeping dressed meat, one was compelled to transport live cattle. Now, to transport alive a steer of 500 kilograms, results in transporting at least 250 kilograms of bone, horns, hoofs, hide, and entrails. These parts undoubtedly have some value, but in the field they will have, notwithstanding the measures taken by the administration, little or no value. To these objections others are to be added, such as the transportation of the forage, the subsistence of the herders, and the difficulty of loading and unloading these heavy animals.

"From all these considerations it follows at least that the cattle cannot be transported on the hoof; they should be slaughtered, cut up, and loaded on cars, boats, or wagons. The problem is not difficult to solve, since at the present time dressed meat is forwarded from South America to London and in a perfect state of preservation, notwithstanding a voyage of forty-five days.

"As concerns the supply for fortresses, it should be composed chiefly of preserved meats. When one has seen the difficulties that a commandant of a fortress experiences to hold, feed, and keep in good condition a large herd, the ravages caused by the cattle plague, the shells from the enemy's artillery which set fire to the stables, one gains convincing proof that, even in a large fortress, protected by detached works, it is possible to keep alive cattle only during the beginning of the investment, and that preserves of meat should, in the future, always be used in constituting the supplies for a siege."—*Pierron*, "*Stratégie et Grande Tactique,*" Vol. III., p. 67.

"Advantages of Transporting Dressed Meats," by M. TELLIER:

"Animals transported on foot or in cars suffer from lack of food and water, from the disturbance caused in their manner of life, from the uneasiness caused by fright and crowding in the cars. Thus they arrive, if not sick, at least in an unhealthy condition.

"When slaughtered at the places of production, the animal is killed, on the other hand, in the best condition. The meat is healthy, nourishing, and the following advantages are obtained: the offal of the animal serves for manure; the hides supply the local industry; the transports are loaded only with edible meat.

"To assure good keeping qualities to dressed meat, it is not necessary to resort to chemical ingredients, cold itself gives a satisfactory result, or, rather, the temperature of 32° F., without variation and in perfectly dry air. If the temperature is above 32° F., the meat does not keep; if it is below, it loses its flavor. With a temperature of 32° F., the result of the conservation is such that at the end of a week the meat is entirely improved, and that it is possible to keep it in that way for two months and longer."—*Pierron*, "*Stratégie et Grande Tactique,*" Vol. III., p. 304

Prussian General VON DER GOLTZ, Inspector of the Line of Communications of the III German Army in 1870–1871:

"In the month of September, 1870, the German Army received a decided check by the appearance of the cattle plague, which compelled it to discontinue all consignments of cattle from the mother country and to be satisfied with what was found in the country, outside the roads traversed by the troops or their trains, and to resort to mutton. The greatest efforts were made to localize the epidemic, but without success; for *the root of the evil was the bad or insufficient nourishment, the lack of care, and the filth of the animals held in enormous herds;* and very often the epidemic appeared rather as the *typhus of hunger* than as the cattle plague. On the road followed by the army it was not possible to find any longer sufficient resources to keep in good condition such large herds, because both friend and foe had exhausted them; on this account herds of about two thousand head of cattle perished in a few days. All that could be done was to separate the healthy cattle from those which were contaminated, to kill the first in order to use them as salt meat, and to bury the others

"The administration of the occupied territories exerted every effort to check the propagation of the epidemic, in order to protect the resources of the country, and it was successful to a considerable degree.

"Later, it was decided to transport the cattle by rail instead of forwarding them by the roads, so as to avoid the localities infected with the cattle plague. But very soon the impossibility of feeding such large numbers of cattle was made manifest, and the typhus of hunger again made its appearance. Finally, it was determined to send from the mother country only bacon, salted or smoked meat, canned foods, and pea sausages, of which the manufacture of large numbers was undertaken."—*Pierron, "Stratégie et Grande Tactique," Vol III, p. 329.*

"Necessity for Canned Provisions" (Captain HEUTSCH, German Army, 1881):

"The effectiveness and mobility of an army depend particularly on the manner in which the soldier is nourished; but this last point presents the greatest difficulties, because the armies of the present time are of immense size and move in a more concentrated order than formerly. To supply such masses from the resources of a country is most frequently an impossibility; and it is not possible to drive cattle herds after them without exposure to the danger of the cattle plague

"Effort has been made to remedy these inconveniences in two ways: by the introduction of preserves as one way, and for another by adopting various methods of freezing in order to transport the dressed meat without its spoiling "—*Pierron, "Stratégie et Grande Tactique," Vol. III, p. 61.*

Sous-Intendant DUSSUTOUR, 1888:

"The enormous herds of the River Plate, of Australia and of New Zealand, were generally used, until recent years, only for the hides and fat of the animals. The meat, in reality, was too abundant to be consumed there, and the methods of preservation too defective to practically permit exportation But on account of the invention of English machines which produce cold, without employing any chemical substance, simply by the compression and quick expansion of air, it is possible to transport now to Europe the meat coming from the large cattle-raising countries.

* * * * * * * * *

"The problem of keeping and transportation of large quantities of meat and supplies appears then successfully solved. The duration of the conservation, moreover, does not appear to be limited; all the experiments made in that respect are entirely conclusive.

* * * * * * * * *

"In wars of the future, the resources of the country occupied will be quickly exhausted by the immense modern armies; and, after a certain length of time, all or nearly all the supplies will be drawn from the adjoining districts or from the interior. Under such conditions frozen meats offer the greatest advantages for supplies. They will be still more valuable for fortified places, if these have been provided with refrigerating machines in time of peace, for the cattle could be slaughtered as soon as the investment is completed, and thus the difficulty of feeding them during the siege would be removed."—*Pierron, "Stratégie et Grande Tactique," Vol. III., p. 79.*

"Études de Guerre, Tactique de Ravitaillements," par le Général LEWAL, 1889, Tome Second, Chapitre X., p. 47:

"In order to supply the possible insufficiency of the fresh meat to be found in a country, resort was formerly made to cattle on the hoof, to herds marching in rear of the columns. When there was no other means of living, it was necessary to submit to all their inconveniences. Canned meat makes it possible to do away with them and will constitute a great advance in provisioning of armies.

* * * * * * * * *

"Marshal DAVOUST wrote to the Chief of Staff on April 3, 1807: 'The cattle plague prevails in our cantonments and has carried off a large number of horned cattle and swine. From a report made to General Friant, of the fifty-six animals which were in his herd, forty-nine died in twenty-four hours.' Marshal DAVOUST again wrote to the Emperor from Skierniewice, on September 21, 1807: 'The Intendant-général has reported a quantity of beef on the hoof, which should be sufficient for six months' consumption; but the loss of a large number of animals on the road and the great loss in weight of those which arrive reduced the supply reported more than one-half; and this is under the supposition that the cattle plague does not attack our herds, but for the past month it has made the greatest ravages, and we are about to experience the greatest embarrassment.'

"Frequent mention has been made of the typhus, which so cruelly afflicted the garrison of Dresden and all of Germany in 1813. The origin of it has been traced to the diseased cattle drawn from Hungary by the Austrian Army.

"The Germans in 1870 saw the cattle plague break out in their herds at Sarrelouis, Courcelles, Ars, Jouy, etc. It was necessary to slaughter at one time a thousand head, to take the most severe sanitary measures, and the supply of fresh meat soon became nearly impossible.

"Such instances should cause serious consideration for the future, when the dangers will increase with the numbers. From this may come the cattle plague, carbuncles, typhus, cholera, and these plagues may assume a very dangerous form in the enormous numbers of future armies.

* * * * * * * * *

"Thus the animals passing from one corral to another, or following the columns, are continuously on the move, and marching injures them

"The same old stereotyped phrase is reproduced in all the courses of lectures on administration 'Meat is a food which marches' It indeed marches too much

"With large armies the fresh meat must necessarily be brought from a great distance in rear The railroads will relieve the animals of a portion of the distance, but not of the fatigues of the journey In the trains they will suffer greatly from hunger and thirst; they are crowded, frightened, constant prey to disease, accidents are numerous

"Immediately on disembarkation, the cattle are rapidly forwarded to the troops. They are driven at quick and unusual pace, and the roads break up their hoofs, which have become accustomed to the softer grounds of the fields and ranges

"A sustained pace is not natural for them. They need frequent and prolonged halts in order to graze and particularly to ruminate Instead of this, the herders and the dogs urge them forward and harass them

"The cattle are driven all day and halt for a short time in corrals, rarely in pastures Their nourishment, always insufficient, is often not supplied at all The mortality in the herds on the march is frightful, and those that survive the hardships of the march are emaciated and scarcely more than skin and bones The proportion of this thin, tough meat, nearly always diseased, to bones, tendons, and cartilage, falls to 50 or 60 per cent and sometimes more If this is not considered, the nutritive value of the ration is thus considerably reduced, and to raise it the expense would be greatly increased "

"Marshal DAVOUST to the Emperor (Warsaw, November 12, 1807): 'I have written to the Intendant and have advised him, instead of making consignments of cattle, to send here the value of these cattle The loss the cattle undergo which are forwarded to us by the Intendant, either from lack of nourishment, or from epizooty, increases the price of those that arrive to the price of 40 sols per pound (instead of 7), and then this meat is thin and the very worst quality.'

"These serious objections to cattle on the hoof are not the only ones. The herd marches much slower than the troops If they follow the troops, they will not complete the day's march until an hour or two after the rear of the column, if they are started with the advance guard, they are overtaken in time by the column, they raise clouds of dust, are a great hindrance, and give rise to disorder and confusion. Actuated by the necessity for water, food, and rest, and liable to be stampeded, the animals become separated, and then the tiresome work of rounding them up falls upon the men.

"All these disadvantages, apparent in small columns, assume an infinite strength in large ones, they become so potent that cattle on the hoof is a delusion in war of large masses

"The experience of the Germans, in their war relatively easy in so rich a country as France, has demonstrated to them the manifest evils of cattle on the hoof and has induced them to include in their supplies canned meats "

Extract from work entitled "The Army Ration," by E. N.

HORSFORD, late Rumford Professor in Harvard University, Cambridge, Mass., published in 1864, pages 19, 20, and 21:

"Fresh beef as a source of the marching ration has some advantages: it carries itself, the cattle can be driven, but this advantage is limited. Of what use are live cattle on such an expedition as Averill's, to cut the Virginia & Tennessee Railroad; or Kilpatrick's, in the rear of Lee's army, threatening Richmond? In a forced march the herd of cattle must be some distance in the rear, and the supply of fresh beef irregular. The best of cattle in Ohio, Indiana, or Illinois, after transportation in cars, with little water, food, or sleep, during several days and nights of continuous travel, and after being driven about for two or three weeks, with scanty forage or none at all, furnish as a whole meager and inferior beef. To preserve the beef, the cattle are slaughtered—in summer, early in the morning—and the meat immediately boiled, if conveniences will permit, to prevent its becoming fly-blown. The juices extracted in the boiling are uniformly and necessarily lost. The edible meat is much of it lost in the difficulty and haste of detaching it from the bones; it has no provision against spontaneous decay, it is not always at command when most needed; it is bulky, and yet the actual edible meat which the soldier derives from an ox slaughtered on the march is much less than is ordinarily supposed. The advantage of providing it on the hoof is correspondingly small.

"In slaughtering, the weight is diminished by loss of blood, the removal of the tongue, heart, and liver, the viscera and offal, and legs to the knee. This reduction, called 'shrinkage,' in good cattle fresh from the pasture amounts to at least one-third. An ox in fair condition, weighing 1,500 pounds on the hoof, would lose by shrinkage 500 pounds.

* * * * * * * *

"A medical officer, whose duties called him to Chattanooga during the months preceding the battle of Lookout Mountain, has informed me that the cattle furnished to that post were so sick and exhausted from the effects of the transportation from Louisville, and so reduced and emaciated from having had absolutely nothing to eat on the railroad and after their arrival, *for weeks* in succession, that some of them reeled in walking, and, falling or lying down, were unable to rise. It is true that the bullocks that thus fell were not eaten, but they indicate the condition of those which had been subjected to the same suffering and deprivations and were actually used as food. What these cattle on the hoof cost the Government I know not, but probably not less than the cattle supplied to the Army of the Potomac, while their value for food must have been less and the cost of the ration of fresh beef correspondingly greater."

CANNED MEAT.—"The impossibility of driving cattle, the necessity for a food always ready, even without fire, in battle, on the march, in bivouac, and at the outposts, has compelled the adoption of canned meat and vegetables of commerce for the supply of troops in the field."—*Lewal*, "*Etudes de Guerre,*" Tome II, *p.* 52.

"Cours Professés à l'École d'Administration Militaire de Vincennes, pendant l'Année 1891," Volume II., page 343:

"Such a reserve—*i. e.*, of cattle herds—imposed upon the contractor entails a heavy charge against the Treasury, which pays the interest on the capital invested; it also deprives the cavalry of all the forage consumed on the spot by the cattle. These inconveniences have suggested the idea of utilizing for the supply of fresh meat for armies a very recent discovery which permits the transportation to great distances of dressed meats after having frozen them. In the field, if too serious obstacles are not encountered, this system is destined to render important services and to effect great economies It is being investigated at present with the view of its application to the supply of fortresses; undoubtedly the same investigation will be extended to the question of the supply of fresh meat in the field."

General PIERRON, in his work entitled "Statégie et Grande Tactique d'après l'Experience des Dernières Guerres," Volume III., page 4, states:

"As a campaign would not be entered into without a plan of operations, it is likewise necessary to previously form the plan of supply to provide the subsistence for the soldier and for the horse in the zone of concentration:

"The questions to be solved are the following:

* * * * * * * * *

"8. Where should the large slaughter-houses be established?" and answers as follows:

"8. The large slaughter-houses will forward to the army the meat cut up and preserved, either by the use of ice or by means of air or industrial process. They will be located near the railway, in a locality abounding in forage and water, where the large enclosures will make 'it possible to keep the cattle in healthy condition.' "—*Id., p.* 6.

"Although the supply of fresh meats for armies is a relatively easy matter on account of the great abundance of cattle in all portions of the country and of means of transportation, the danger from distempers subject the administration to the greatest inconveniences.

"When toward the end of the month of August, 1870, the 1st German Army had united with the 2d in the investment of Metz, the cattle plague broke out in the herds assembled at Sarrelouis, Courcelles, Ars, and Jouy, and caused great ravages in a few days. The army could count neither on the local resources, since it was to remain in the same place for an indefinite period, nor upon those of the zones in the rear, for the cattle forwarded would have been rapidly contaminated and would have served only to increase the extent of the contagion. It was necessary to establish at Mayence a field *abattoir*, from which the quarters of dressed meat previously washed, dried, and salted in order to assure the keeping qualities, then surrounded with straw, were forwarded directly to the troops by the railway.

"Since that time an industry has been developed, which, under similar conditions, would be of great assistance to armies in the field. We now refer to the preservation of meats by *cold and dry air*.

"You know that this is the method adopted by breeders of La Plata, of Australia, etc., who until recently could only utilize the fat and hides of their herds to import to Europe immense quantities of meat. In France also a cold-storage depot has been installed at Havre, and sends each week to Paris 2,000 carcasses of mutton and the same number of quarters of beef The meat, after having been dried, is placed in a refrigerating chamber with double walls, where a current of cold air, produced by a refrigerating machine, maintains the necessary temperature.

The frozen meat is transported by rail, in cars specially constructed, where, efore starting, the cold air necessary to keep the meat in good condition during the journey, is introduced.

"The frozen meat needs no preparation before being used, it is sufficient to hang it in dry air for some time to bring it to the temperature of the surrounding air and permit it to regain all its natural qualities. In summer twelve hours are sufficient to obtain this result; in winter some hours longer are necessary."—*Crétin,* "*Conférences sur l'Administration Militaire,*" *p.* 420.

"The Organization and Administration of the Lines of Communication in War," by Colonel GEORGE ARMAND FURSE, C. B., London, 1894, page 279:

* * * * * * * * *

"Cattle can be driven in every direction the troops have to take; this is supposed to render the service of the meat ration more easy and manageable than any other. We must, nevertheless, take into account that the animals often follow the columns with difficulty, and that long marches of numerous herds of cattle, with the grazing often limited and of inferior quality, have the effect of lowering the condition of the animals and of abstracting from their flesh some of its nutritive qualities. As a rule, cattle should always be rested for some hours before being slaughtered

"Proper steps must be taken in time to provide against any failure in the supply of cattle for slaughter, for this, unfortunately, is one of the supplies which fails first. If the occupied territory cannot supply cattle in sufficient number, they must be obtained from foreign markets. The purchase of cattle, however, requires judgment, for we read in ancient history (A. D 810) how the cattle plague destroyed all the cattle the Emperor Charlemagne had collected for his army Coming down to more recent times, Sir W. Power remarks: 'Epidemics almost invariably occur in countries where there is such unusual movement of cattle as is caused in war. In Roumania, Bulgaria, and Asia Minor, during the Crimean War, murrain amongst the sheep and cattle became almost universal, and it spread into the principalities before the war was ended It is a well-established fact that the cattle purchased in Russia and Poland for the German Army in the War of 1870-1871 brought the cattle plague into the Prussian Provinces

* * * * * * * * *

"PRESERVED PROVISIONS —When the supply of animals for slaughter is very uncertain, or when bad or insufficient forage or water prevent the cattle from following the troops, these will have to be fed on canned or salted meats The soldier always prefers the more familiar forms of food, and the patent compounds and preserved provisions that replace them are not unnaturally unpopular with him.—*Idem, p.* 282

* * * * * * * * *

"Canned meat, salted beef or pork, demand a large increase in the transport, as only fresh meat carries itself The long droves of live cattle are, however, a source of constant delay, in certain instances the enfeeblement of the animals performing long marches with insufficient time for grazing, and the conditions under which they are slaughtered and cut up, are greatly against their being used. In such cases, but for the precaution of keeping a large supply of preserved provisions handy, the soldier would have to go without meat.

"The great progress made in late years in the preservation of food has been of signal advantage in the alimentation of troops in the field. Canned meats and biscuit pack well, keep for a long period, and are not subject to the same deterioration as fresh provisions; preserved provisions can be eaten at once, and, their weight being uniform, the distributions can be made with greater speed and less labor. The meat has no bone; all is useful food. With respect to packing, every care should be taken to reduce the bulk on account of the saving it will effect in the transport.

"Notwithstanding the many advantages claimed for preserved provisions, they should only be considered in the light of a reserve, to be used when necessity compels us to resort to these substitutes, for fresh bread and fresh meat are necessary to secure the health and strength of the soldier Reasonable as it is to take into account the many difficulties which encompass the procuring of fresh eatables for the troops, to imagine that an unlimited use of preserved provisions can be made during a campaign is a fallacy to be judiciously guarded against. As nothing is considered more conducive to the maintenance of health than a change of diet, every effort must be made to obtain at all times as large a supply of fresh provisions as possible. The stomach demands a change of diet; after many days of feeding on boiled meat, everyone knows what a relief it is to be able to partake of a bit of roast flesh

"With regard to a too prolonged use of preserved provisions, it should be observed that when the soldier is in comfortable quarters and has comparatively light work to perform, he is fed on bread, fresh meat, vegetables, and groceries; when, on the other hand, in the field, he has to undergo fatiguing marches—carrying a heavy weight—and is subject to every kind of exposure, necessity often compels us to feed him on hard biscuit and preserved meat. Thus, when his nourishment requires to be of the best is the very time when he ceases to partake of the most strengthening food.

"It is more economical to supply canned meat in small tins; when issued in six-pound tins, a great part of it is thrown away and wasted. It has been found that the meat in tins which have been exposed to a very hot sun has gone bad.

"Canned meat is very devoid of fat, consequently after a short time it becomes distasteful. Some kinds being more salted than others, preference should be given to the less salted sorts in operations conducted in countries where the water supply is known to be limited. Smoked meat retains all its nutritive constituents, and is therefore preferable to salt meat. The brine in the preparation of the latter abstracts many of the substances which are essential to the constitution of the flesh, thus salted meat in process of salting becomes deficient of nutritive materials, and is injurious when it forms a principal and continuous article of diet."

"Alimentation et Ravitaillement des Armées en Campagne, Cours d'Administration en temps de guerre et de manœuvres professé à l'Ecole Supérieure de Guerre en 1896–1897," par M. PEYROLLE, Sous-Intendant Militaire de 1re classe, page 88:

"At the end of August (1870) an epidemic broke out in the herds at Sarrelouis, Courcelles, Ars-sur-Moselle, Puy-aux-Arches It became necessary to slaughter the cattle and supply the army investing Metz only with smoked or salted meat The troops becoming tired of it, there was an *abattoir* established at Mayence, from which was forwarded meat packed in straw, which had previously been cooked and rubbed with pepper and salt; but this bred dysentery."

"Provisioning Armies in the Field," by Colonel GEORGE ARMAND FURSE, C. B., London, 1899, page 292:

* * * * * * * * *

"Nothing will so conduce to the health and strength of the fighting man as fresh bread and fresh meat; this is incontestable; nevertheless, fresh provisions occupy a good deal of room and are easily spoilt. Say that the soldier has been furnished with a supply for three days, the whole of his haversack will be nearly filled, causing him inconvenience. The meat portion carried in a haversack with a number of other articles soon gets tainted and loathsome; it turns equally bad if carried in a mess-tin. At the commencement of a march, the soldier will possibly strive to keep the rations in good condition, but little by little he will become careless. If it becomes very hot, if dust gets at the haversack, the meat is spoilt; a great portion of it becomes unpalatable and is cast away.

"Meat is often said to be the only part of the soldier's food which carries itself; in other words, herds of cattle follow the march of the troops. How badly fitted the animals must be for food after a march of from twelve to fifteen miles a day, smothered by dust, without proper pasture and water, can be left to imagination. Under these disadvantages the cattle cannot but lose condition, and cattle much out of condition are liable to take and spread all manner of contagious diseases Animals obtained locally on requisition or by purchase will be in better condition for slaughter.

"The rule with regard to live stock is that the vital energy of the animals which may have been to any extent impaired by excessive fatigue or from any other cause, should have fully recovered before they are slaughtered; then only the flesh can be considered of good quality. This condition is not fulfilled with cattle which have to conform to the movements of the troops. Their habits of life are totally changed: accustomed to wander leisurely on soft fields, on the march they tread on hard roads, urged at a pace to them extraordinary; they are pressed for many consecutive hours; are harassed and kept in a feverish condition. The animals will be saved much fatigue when transported part of the way by rail; nevertheless this will not spare them the hardships of the journey. They will be overcrowded, seriously frightened, and will suffer from exposure, hunger, and thirst.

"To drive cattle on the hoof in rear of the combatants is, by many practical men, regarded as an error. As cattle march slower than the troops, they cause intervals in the length of the column; they are difficult to keep together on such roads as are not bound by fences, and come into camp long after the troops; there they are penned up, and seldom get an opportunity for picking up food in pasture-fields. Under these conditions the animals soon get reduced to skin and bone, and the nutritive value of the ration is very considerably lowered. Should the animals show signs of having contracted any contagious disease, they will have to be destroyed, without having rendered any service to the commissariat

* * * * * * * * *

"The need for driving cattle no longer exists, now that preserved meat of good quality and at a resonable price has become an article of commerce.

"Preserved provisions of many kinds have now come to be of the greatest help to an army in the field. Both with regard to their transportation and employment, they are very well adapted for use in a campaign. Preserved provisions rank as *reserves;* the principal conditions which these eatables should fulfil are: good nutritive qualities, small volume, lightness, good keeping qualities, and speediness in the preparation of the meals.

"Provisions of this kind occupy less space and weigh less than fresh victuals; they enable the soldier to live for a certain number of days on what he carries in his valise, if the country he is in affords no other resources, or the army has outstripped its provision columns. When the local resources are insufficient to provide all that is needed, by adding preserved provisions to the little that is found the soldier can be adequately fed. The advantages of preserved meat and preserved vegetables have been so fully recognized that in most European States, with a view to their employment in war, establishments have been provided for their manufacture.

"What is much to be desired in many of the circumstances of a campaign is a description of eatables which can be easily transported and have beyond doubt good keeping qualities. A reserve ration, small in bulk, very nourishing, and easy to transport, which, when substituted for the ordinary provisions, should give an invigorating meal. Certain rapid and continuous movements cannot be executed without something of this sort.

"When employing railways as lines of supplies, a very ordinary reflection will show how a certain number of trucks will be able to carry far more rations of preserved meat than their equivalent in live cattle. Indeed, all the many experiences which have been made with substitutes for fresh meat have had, amongst other principal objects, a tangible reduction in the matter of transport. In the field, however, it is held that their use should not be pushed too far, for a lengthy consumption of any single description of food tires and disgusts the stomach. Man, not satisfied with procuring food for his support, has endeavored to add to it some seasoning which will gratify his palate. In the Franco-German War the German soldiers very frequently complained that they were tired of the same nourishment; that there was no variety, no account taken of their taste.

"Canned meat has several advantages. It can be carried by the soldier for any time without undergoing deterioration; it nourishes him well, for a pound of it really represents a pound of food; it is more tender than freshly killed meat; it can be made into excellent soup or can be eaten cold. This last is a very valuable advantage when the soldier has not time to cook his meals on service, has no fuel, or is worn down by fatigue. He can then eat a piece of it cold with some bread or biscuit, and soon lie down to take his rest. Compare this with the use of fresh provisions when, to prepare a meal, water and fuel have to be fetched, the fires lighted, and some hours must naturally be allowed to elapse before the food is cooked and fit to eat.

"But, invaluable an article as canned meat is for troops in the field, it is devoid of fat, and soldiers quickly tire of it. The point which should engage our attention is to study how it can be made the basis of a really palatable meal. The chief point in this direction is to assimilate the nourishment to what the soldier has been accustomed to in his home. With a

little ingenuity, several ways will be found of cooking canned meat, and when mixed with certain ordinary essences and condiments—extracts of onions, celery, carrots, parsley, etc.—some way may be discovered that will deprive it of its somewhat insipid taste. Onions are invaluable; they impart an agreeable flavor to the soup. Rice, lentils, pearl barley, or oatmeal, added to it, would have that effect. These articles keep well."—
Idem, pp. 294, 295

The Supply Service in the Field. From the Point of View of the Staff of the Higher Commands by COLONEL V. FRANCOIS, Chief of the General Staff of the IVth (German) Army Corps Part I, 1904, Page 27.

The "Dienstanweisung für den Schlachtereibetrieb und den Viehtransport" ("Regulations for the Slaughtering and Transport of Animals") states that pigs, calves, and cattle ready for killing cannot undertake long marches, and that they can only be moved long distances overland by means of box wagons. The regulations lay down the distance that oxen can march in a day as 20 kilometers on the average, provided that there are two rest days in each week and that the animals are well fed and looked after. Oxen and pigs will therefore have to be left behind when troops are continually advancing, and cannot, as a rule, be used in such circumstances for supply purposes. Any attempts to make the animals march further might easily lead to the outbreak of all sorts of diseases These animals have but little stamina; when they have to endure much physical exertion and are badly looked after and insufficiently fed, they die and their carcases poison the air. The conditions under which sheep can be forwarded are much more favorable. "The Regulations for the Slaughtering and Transport of Animals" gauges their average marching powers at 30 kilometers per diem. According to this, their rate of movement is approximately the same as that of the troops; flocks of sheep could therefore be driven along and made use of for feeding purposes.

"*Les Principes du Ravitaillement des Armées Modernes, Appliqués à la Guerre Russo-Japonaise,*" par l' Intendant Militaire Jean Schrabök, du Comité Militaire Technique Austro-Hongrois.

"In the particular part of Manchuria then occupied, no beef cattle are raised. The Chinaman eats no beef and makes no use of dairy products. Cattle are used only as draft animals and they are not found in great numbers. In Mongolia, on the contrary, the raising of beef cattle is one of the principal industries; but Chinese neutrality interposed an obstacle to purchase of supplies in that province, and it became necessary to employ, for this purpose, persons who were on friendly terms with the Mongol princes.

"There were, however, drawbacks to the plan of buying beeves at so great a distance. It required a large escort to drive and care for the animals, and it was besides necessary to vaccinate the droves against splenic fever, in order that the men themselves might not contract the disease. This required the procuring and keeping on hand of sufficient quantity of the specific serum. Finally, the watering of any considerable number of animals presented great difficulties, particularly in winter. To all these complications was added the rapid increase of troops, which suddenly aggravated the conditions.

"The approach of the cold season had likewise given rise to orders for frozen beef to be shipped from the rear, though this measure produced but a tardy effect. There were, besides, serious losses resulting from accidents on the railway."

From the "Revue du Service de l' Intendance Militaire," Tome XX., p. 881.

BIBLIOGRAPHY.

"Aide-Mémoire de l'Officier d'Etat-Major en Campagne." Paris, Henri Charles-Lavauzelle.

Arnold, Captain.
"Die Tätigkeit des Verpflegsoffiziers in Zusammenhang mit den militärischen Operationen." Oldenburg, Gerhard Stalling, 1908.

Aubry, Ch., Sous-Intendant Militaire.
"Le Ravitaillement des Armées de Frédéric-le-Grand et de Napoléon." Paris, Henri Charles-Lavauzelle.

Audouin, Xavier.
"Histoire de l'Administration Militaire de la Guerre." Quatre tomes. Paris, P. Didot l'ainé, 1811.

Ballyet, M., Intendant Militaire.
"De la Constitution de l'Administration Militaire en France." Paris, 1817.

Baratier, A., Intendant Militaire.
"Etude sur la Campagne de 1806-1807, au point de vue de service des subsistances." Paris, 1888.
"L'Administration Militaire au Tonkin." Paris, 1888 and 1889.
"Principes Rationnels de la Marche des Impedimenta dans les Grandes Armées." Paris, J. Dumaine, 1872.
"L'Art de Ravitailler les Grandes Armées." J. Dumaine, 1874. (Out of print.)
"Essai d'Instruction sur la Subsistance des Troupes en Campagne dans le Service de Première Ligne." J. Dumaine, 1875. (Out of print.)

Barber, Captain R., A. S. C.
"The Supply and Transport of the Japanese Army as Far as the Yalu River." *Army Service Corps Quarterly*, Vol. II., 1907-1908.

Blanchenay, M., Intendant Militaire.
"Note sur l'Exécution du Service de l'Intendance pendant les Opérations sur la Frontière Marocaine (1907-1908)." *Revue du Service de l'Intendance Militaire*, Vol. XXI., 1908.

Boissonnet, M., Sous-Intendant Militaire en retraite.
"Approvisionnement de Siège de Paris." Paris, 1890.

Boissonnet, Lieutenant-Colonel.
"L'Entretien des Armées." Paris, Berger, Levrault et Cie., 1907.

Boysson, M. de, Contrôleur de l'Administration de l'Armée.
"Note sur l'Emploi des Locomotives Routières et les Pétrins Mécaniques pour les Boulangeries de Campagne." Paris, 1888.

Buxton, Major J. W.
"The Elements of Military Administration." London, Kegan Paul, Trench, Trübner & Co., 1883.

Clayton, Lieutenant-Colonel F. T.
"Supply of an Army in the Field." London, Edward Stanford, 1899.

"Cours Professés à l'Ecole d'Administration Militaire de Vincennes, pendant l'Année 1891." Deux tomes   Paris, Henri Charles-Lavauzelle, 1891.

Crétin, Ch
"Conférences sur l'Administration Militaire Faites à l'Ecole Supérieure de Guerre." Paris, Berger-Levrault et Cie., 1889

Cumberlege, Captain H C F., A S C
"Requisitions in War"   *Army Service Corps Quarterly*, Vol I , 1905-1907.
"The Raison d'Etre of Permanent Supply and Transport Establishments"   *Journal of the Royal United Service Institution*, Vol L , August and September, 1906; also *Army Service Corps Quarterly*, Vol. I., 1905-1907

de Fonblanque, Edward Barrington.
"Treatise on the Administration and Organization of the British Army, with Especial Reference to Finance and Supply." London, Longmans, Brown & Co , 1858

Dupain, M , Sous-Intendant Militaire de 2e classe.
"L'Administration Militaire Austro-hongroise, son organisation et son fonctionnement en temps de paix et en temps de guerre." Paris, 1892
"L'Administration Militaire Italienne, son organisation et son fonctionnement en temps de paix et en temps de guerre " Paris, 1892.
"L'Intendance Militaire Allemande et les Services qui en Dépendent; leur organisation et leur fonctionnement en temps de paix et en temps de guerre." Paris, 1891.

Dusutour, H , Sous-Intendant Militaire
"Conservation des Viandes à l'Etat Naturel par l'Air Froid et Sec; application du système à l'alimentation de l'Armée " Paris, 1888.

Espanet, M., Sous-Intendant Militaire de 3e classe.
"Etude sur le Fonctionnement de la Boulangerie de Campagne d'un Corps d'Armée " Paris, 1892.

Espanet, O.
"Notes on the Supply of an Army during Active Operations " Kansas City, Mo , Hudson–Kimberly Publishing Company, 1899
"Etudes sur le Service des Etapes d'après les Renseignments Personnels Récueillis pendant la Guerre de 1870-71," par un officier l'Inspection Générale Bavaroise des Etapes   Traduit de l'allemand par Couturier, Lieutenant au 55e régiment   Paris, Ch Tanera, 1872

Ferrand, Georges.
"Des Réquisitions Militaires   Etudes d'Administration Militaire au point de vue du droit des gens et du droit public français " Paris, L. Baudoin, 1892.

Fortescue, Hon. J. W.
"Transport and Supply "   *United Service Magazine* (London), Vol. XXVIII , November and December, 1903: January, 1904

Frédéric-le-Grand, Roi de Prusse.
"L'Art de la Guerre."   Poème en six chants.   Ouvrage retouché par Voltaire, sous les yeux du Monarque, et accompagné d'une Préface d'arguments et de notes par M Louis du Bois, membre de plusieurs Académies de Paris, etc., à Paris, chez Anselin, 1830

Furse, George Armand, Lieutenant-Colonel
"Military Transport "   London, William Clowes & Sons, 1882

"Mobilization and Embarkation of an Army Corps." London, William Clowes & Sons, 1883.

Furse, George Armand, Colonel, C. B.
"The Organization and Administration of the Lines of Communication in War." London, William Clowes & Sons, 1894.
"Military Expeditions Beyond the Seas." In two volumes. London, William Clowes & Sons, 1897.
"Provisioning Armies in the Field." London, William Clowes & Sons, 1899.

Gaillard, J. B., Intendant Général.
"Etude sur le Service de l'Intendance Militaire en Campagne." Rédigée en 1860. Paris, Levenen, 1863.

Gauldrée-Boilleau, Adolphe.
"L'Administration Militaire dans les Temps Modernes." Paris, J. Dumaine, 1879.
"L'Administration Militaire dans l'Antiquité." Paris, J. Dumaine, 1871.

Gervais, A.
"L'Alimentation dans l'Armée." Paris, L. Baudoin, 1894.

Haking, Colonel R., C. B.
"Staff Rides and Regimental Tours." London, Hugh Rees (Limited), 1908.

Kirn, Léon, Capitaine au 20e régiment territorial d'Infanterie.
"L'Alimentation du Soldat." Paris, L. Baudoin, 1885.

Kottié, J.-N., Ritter v., Général Intendant dans l'Armée autrichienne.
"De l'Emploi de la Contribution en Nature comme Mode d'Alimentation des Armées en Campagne." Groz, Librairie Styria, 1890. Préface par M. Dufour, sous-intendant militaire. Paris, 1890.

Landwehr von Pragenau, Captain, General Staff Corps.
"Ueber den Turnus der Verpflegungsstaffeln."
"Mitteilungen über Gegenstände des Artillerie- und Geniewesens." December, 1904.

Laymann, Major-General.
"Die Mitwirkung der Truppe bei der Ernährung der Millionenheere des nächsten Krieges." Berlin, Hermann Walther, 1907.

Le Mesurier, Thomas Augustus, Lieutenant-Colonel.
"The Feeding of Fighting Armies." Harrison & Sons, London, 1904.

Lewal, le Général.
"Etudes de Guerre. Tactique des Ravitaillements." Deux tomes. Paris, L. Baudoin et Cie., 1889.
"Stratégie de Marche." Paris, L. Baudoin, 1893.

Malvy, M., Sous-Intendant Militaire.
"L'Alimentation des Armées en Campagne." Conférence de garnison. Paris, 1897.

Napier-Nunn, Captain C. H., A. S. C.
"Army Service Corps Duties on a Staff Ride, Outlines of." *Army Service Corps Quarterly*, Vol. I., 1905-1907.

Ned-Noll.
"Etude sur la Tactique de Ravitaillement dans les Guerres Coloniales." Paris, Henri Charles-Lavauzelle, 1895.

Odier, P. A., Sous-Intendant Militaire.
"Cours d'Etudes sur l'Administration Militaire." Sept tomes. Paris, Anselin et Pochard, 1824.

Pernot, A.
"Aperçu Historique sur le Service des Transports Militaires." Paris, Henri Charles-Lavauzelle, 1894.

Pérot, M. A., Sous-Intendant Militaire de 2e classe.
"Emploi du Chemin de Fer à voie de 0m. 60 pour Ravitaillement des Troupes." Paris, 1895.
"Administration, Contributions et Réquisitions Allemandes dans le Department de l'Aube en 1870-1871." Paris, 1899.

Peyrolle, M., Sous-Intendant Militaire.
"Alimentation et Ravitaillement des Armées en Campagnes." Cours d'Administration en temps de guerre et de manœuvres, professé à l'Ecole Supérieure de Guerre, en 1896-1897. Paris, Henri Charles-Lavauzelle.
"De l'Alimentation des Troupes en Campagne. Comparaison des systèmes français et allemand." Conférence de garnison. Paris, 1891.

Pierron, le Général.
"Stratégie et Grande Tactique d'après l'Expérience des Dernières Guerres." Trois tomes. Paris, Berger-Levrault et Cie, 1887.

Quitteray, M., Sous-Intendant Militaire de la 1re classe.
"L'Alimentation des Troupes en Campagne." Une conférence de garnison. Paris, 1892.

Roguet, Général de brigade.
"De l'Approvisionnement des Armées au XIXme Siècle." Paris, J. Dumaine, 1848.

Roguet, Lieutenant-Général Comte
"Mémoires Militaires de" Quatre tomes. Paris, L. Baudoin, 1862

Rupp, M. Charles, Sous-Intendant Militaire à Meaux.
"Revue du Service de l'Intendance Militaire," Vol. XXI., 1908.

Schellendorf, Major-General Bronsart von
"The Duties of the General Staff." Two volumes. London, Henry S. King & Co., 1877.

Schindler, Charles.
"L'Alimentation du Soldat en Campagne. La ration de guerre et la préparation rapide des repas en campagne." Paris, Henri Charles-Lavauzelle, 1887.

Sharpe, H. G., Captain and C S, U. S. A.
"The Art of Subsisting Armies in War." New York, John Wiley & Sons, 1893.
"The Art of Supplying Armies in the Field as Exemplified during the Civil War." Prize Essay, Military Service Institution for 1895. Published in *Journal of the Military Service Institution*, January, 1896.

Sharpe, Henry G., Commissary-General.
"Subsisting Our Field Army in Case of War with a First-Class Power." *Journal of the Military Service Institution of the United States*, Vol. XLIV., May, June, July, and August, 1909.

"Staff Duties." A series of lectures for the use of officers at the Staff College. London, Harrison & Sons, 1890.

"The System under Which Food and Forage Are Supplied to an Army," by Lieutenant-Colonel Grattan, commanding Army Service Corps, Aldershot. Printed in Vol. X (1889) *Journal of the Military Service Institution of the United States*, p. 693.

7—

Thomas, Brevet-Colonel A. H.
"Methods of Feeding Troops in War." Military Society of Ireland. Dublin, 1904.

Thomas, Colonel A. H.
"Some Administrative Duties in War." *Army Service Corps Quarterly*, Vol. I., 1905–1907.

Trémérél, G., et Marullaz, H.
"Aide-Mémoire de l'Officier d'Administration et de l'Officier d'Approvisionnement en Campagne." Paris, Henri Charles-Lavauzelle, 1895.
"Vade-Mecum de l'Officier d'Approvisionnement des Corps de Troupe de Toutes Armes et des Quartiers Généraux." (9e édition.) Paris, Henri Charles-Lavauzelle.

Vauchelle, M., Ancien Intendant Militaire, etc.
"Cours d'Administration Militaire." Quatrième édition. Trois tomes. Paris, J. Dumaine, 1861.

Vigo-Roussillon, M., Intendant Militaire.
"Des Principes de l'Administration des Armées. Deux conférences faites au Ministère de la Guerre le 3 et 10 Mars, 1869. Paris, J. Dumaine, 1871.

von François, Colonel.
"The Supply Service in the Field."
"Feldverpflegungsdienst bei den höheren Kommandobehörden."

Ward, E. W. D., Lieutenant-Colonel, C. B.
"Army Service Corps Duties in Peace and in War." London, Kegan Paul, Trench, Trübner & Co., 1897.

Wolseley, General, Viscount.
"The Soldier's Pocketbook for Field Service." London, MacMillan & Co., latest edition.

BIBLIOLIFE

Old Books Deserve a New Life
www.bibliolife.com

Did you know that you can get most of our titles in our trademark **EasyScript**™ print format? **EasyScript**™ provides readers with a larger than average typeface, for a reading experience that's easier on the eyes.

Did you know that we have an ever-growing collection of books in many languages?

Order online:
www.bibliolife.com/store

Or to exclusively browse our **EasyScript**™ collection:
www.bibliogrande.com

At BiblioLife, we aim to make knowledge more accessible by making thousands of titles available to you – quickly and affordably.

Contact us:
BiblioLife
PO Box 21206
Charleston, SC 29413